CONTENTS

01. WHY SHOULD ONE CONSIDER ONLINE BUSINESS?

The world's changing every day and so are the business opportunities! Today, you can't see increasing number of cyber huts because almost everyone has an easy access to internet. A lot of business models like the cyber huts have been flooded away in the market because of the speed in which our technology is progressing. Gone are those days when kids sought the help of their parents or elders in the neighborhood to complete their school project. Kids seek help from "The Google Guru" today! This is not only limited to children. As adults, we are more dependable on internet for our needs every day! A major chunk of crowd actively uses internet and from the business person perspective, a lot of customers are found on the internet. This is the major reason behind all BIG companies have started paying so much attention to developing their websites, social media management and so on. It's said that, "Any business can become a great business if there's good market for it" Having more than 3 billion users, internet platform is one of the best platforms today to start your business!

"Any business can become a great business if there's good market for it!"

Throughout the history, there has never been an easier and a better time to start an online business then today! With the increasing engagement of people in the internet, this decade is the best time for you to kick start your online business! It took several years for the giant companies like Dell, Tata, Reliance many others to become billion-dollar companies but with the speeding advance in technology, the number of years taken to become a billionaire is surprisingly decreasing! The best example to this is the WhatsApp cofounders Brian Acton and Jan Koum who became billionaires in less than 5 years when Facebook took over WhatsApp for 19 Billion US Dollars in the year 2014. Online business is thus booming than ever now and now is the best time to invest time and money in an online business!

From my experience I would like to say, you don't have to quit your job and start the online business, while continuing your regular job you can start it part time!! Based on the growth you take a call on when you should take it full time.

With my years of experience in the field of online business as an YouTuber, I can tell you some top reasons on why should one consider online business!

1. Online Business is extremely inexpensive!

Unlike the traditional business that requires lots of investment into capital and machinery, online business is extremely cost effective. If you plan to start an YouTube channel, all you'll need is a talent or skill that you wish to share with the world and the related costs for making your video. Getting ideas is easy; real challenge lies in implementing them! If you think about why people back out from implementing their amazing ideas, you'll notice that a lot of them don't implement their business idea simply because they failed to gather the required investment. What could be better news for people than a business opportunity that requires minimal investment? When I started my YouTube channel A2C Arts And Crafts (will be referred as A2C going forward), I invested nothing but my time and mind to think about new ideas with little investment for having a laptop, camera/phone to capture the video, which most of us have these days. My investment has never changed since then! It actually is that easy! If you're looking for a business model that requires least investment but churns out good profits, online business is definitely worth a try!

2. Time saving

You don't need to spend hours together every day in order to get readers or viewers when you consider an online business. There are Youtubers who earn in millions of dollars per year by just spending a day or two in the whole week. Do you think I spend all my time making videos for my channel? The truth is NO, I don't. I do have a regular job on which I spend time from Monday to Friday. Only on weekends, that is, on Saturdays and Sundays do I spend time for making my YouTube videos. This time includes the time spent on idea conceptualizing, shooting my video and editing it! So, it actually takes only 4 to 8 days in a month for me to work on my online business. But then, the best part here is that even when I'm not working, my videos are working for me every day and generating income for me as viewers are looking at my videos! Best part is, I earn more from YouTube channel than my Mon-Friday Job.

*"You don't need to work on your videos for long hours, but these videos are going to work for you 24*7 to generate more views and thus, more income for you!"*

Being a fan of Mr. Robert Kiyosaki, the author of international best seller 'Rich Dad, Poor Dad', I would like to quote his lines, "Don't work for money; Make money work for you!" On the similar lines, you don't need to work on your videos for long hours but these videos are going to work for you 24*7 to generate more views and thus, more income for you!

3. Convenience to the user

The very reason why E-commerce websites like Flipkart/Amazon are a big boom is because of the element of convenience to the buyers. Buyers or customers no longer need to drive or walk to the showroom to purchase clothes or commodities. With online E-commerce websites, shopping has become easier than ever! User convenience will give you an edge! Let's say, you are a pro at cooking and you wish to start your YouTube channel in which you teach making different recipes. You have a competitor who does the same business of teaching how to cook at her home with a classroom environment. Who do you think will have more customers? By all means, it has to be you because in your competitor's case, people need to travel to learn while in your case, they can easily learn from anywhere, anytime!

4. Geographical accessibility: Why limit business with your arm's length customers?

Unlike traditional business models that can attract and retain customers who are at arm's length distance, online business is a great platform allowing you to reach the worldwide market! If you have good number of viewers from all around the globe, there's no stopping you from touching the nooks and corners of the world! Who says, "Location of the business matters a lot for running a good business"? Well, marketing experts do! And they're absolutely right! But it's true only in the context of traditional businesses that require a physical presence. For online business, location is not even a parameter on which business stability can be calculated! The whole world can be your market! (If you know what kind of content must be made which I'll be sharing in the later part of this book)

5. High returns

The old school principle that said, "A business that has high investment has high returns" is outdated now. With the increasing advent of online business, high returns can be churned out even when there's minimal investment. Daniel Middleton (YouTube channel: DanTDM) is the highest 2017 earner of YouTube as per Forbes, with annual earnings of 16.5 Million US Dollars which is more than INR 100 Crores! Now, this amount of money is something that many companies working at an organizational level can only dream of! That's the potential an online business has! PewDiePie is a classic living example to re assure the fact that online business pays off high returns! Statistics has it that the number of YouTube channels that are earning 6 figure amount of money annually is increasing by 50% year on year from 2006! This is exactly why I told you that there can be no better time than now to start an online business or a YouTube Channel to be precise!

6. Flexibility in the time factor

There's immense amount of flexibility with regard to time of the business when it comes to online business. You can upload your blogs or YouTube videos whenever you want! Unlike conventional businesses that have certain timing for business operation, YouTube does not have any sort of timing constraints! Feel like making a video in the middle of the night? Go for it! Make videos at the pace and at the hour you want to and schedule when you want to publish for the audience!

7. Wide Reach

Internet flaunts over 3 billion users which is a wide market for you to grab! With the right video, you can generate millions of viewers quite easily! No other traditional business opportunity can offer you over 3 billion customer base! Thus, online business is definitely worth a try. Of the total 3 billion users, YouTube has over 1 billion users worldwide which is quite a huge amount of crowd or ready viewers! Thus, YouTube can't be referred to as just a source of passive income. If done with the right techniques and right videos, YouTube can act as an active source of income and can help you in earning way more than what you'll need to earn your living!

8. Automation of the business process

Converting a prospective customer into a business deal is a long process that starts with meeting or talking with/to the client, carrying out the sale of product or service, raising the invoice and ends at receiving the amount from the client. This whole process can't get any simpler with online business. All the process is automated and the transactions happening between YouTube and the advertisers who pay the YouTubers (I've explained the payment procedures and the manner in the later part of this book) happen so easily without the direct involvement of the YouTuber. Basically, the entire process is automated and thus you don't have to worry about receiving your payments. All you've got to do is complete your job of uploading content/blogs (in case of a website) and vlogs (in case of YouTube) and work on getting more views. Rest of the job is done by Google AdSense for you! (More explanation on this aspect will be explained in the upcoming chapters)

That was a small list of reasons I can gather from my experience as an

YouTuber as to 'Why one should consider online business' The first step towards starting a YouTube channel is to be totally convinced that investing time here isn't going to go in vain and I think you've gained more conviction now over being an YouTuber! Turn the pages of this book to learn about all you'll need to know in order to come out as a successful YouTuber!

02. HOW CAN YOUTUBE HELP YOU EARN?

Now that you're convinced about why one should consider starting an online business (or YouTube in this context), let's get to know about how YouTube can help people who upload videos on their site earn. This chapter is all about the whole idea on "How does YouTube work?" and how does it benefit the YouTuber (YouTuber is a term used for the person who uploads videos on YouTube). Let's get started!

You would have surely noticed ads coming up in the YouTube videos while you're watching many YouTube video. But is this the case with any video? The answer is NO. Not all the videos have ads coming up. Have you ever wondered why this happens? Well, if you have, I'll tell you why. The videos that have ads coming up are the ones that belong to a channel which has YouTube monetization. In other words, YouTube plays ads on the videos of channels that are eligible for monetization. There are specific eligibility criteria for turning on this feature and once you have turned on monetization as well as fulfilled all the eligibility criteria, you'll start making money for views that your video gets.

Bottom line, there are two conditions that needs to be fulfilled in order to start earning money:

Condition 1 - Turning on the monetization

This is something that many people on YouTube miss out on. There are some people on YouTube who do not turn on monetization option on YouTube. This could be because of three major reasons:

1) The YouTubers do not know that this option needs to be turned on.

They simply go on uploading their videos just out of sheer passion and don't bother to think about monetization of their videos. Most of the people in this category don't know that they don't know!

2) YouTubers who do not intend to make money out of their videos. This crowd unlike the first one knows about monetization of YouTube videos but does not care enough to turn it on because their motto behind uploading videos on YouTube is not for making money. It could be spiritual teachings, psychological channels with people who just want to help out people.

3) YouTubers who create videos and use it to generate money by promoting product sales, personal trainings etc.

Now, depending on the purpose of your videos, you must take a call on whether or not to monetize your videos. If you just wish to give out pure content and don't intend to see YouTube as a source of active or passive income, you can choose not to turn on the monetization option. But if you really want to earn through YouTube and just aren't aware of how it's to be done, don't worry, I've got you covered. In the later part of this book, I've shared the procedure of monetizing your videos.

Condition 2 – How YouTube works and Fulfilling the eligibility criteria for monetization

1st lets understand where's all this money coming from? Let's get to some basic framework.

There are millions of companies that create advertisements and make arrangements with YouTube for playing it on the YouTube videos. These ads are played at the beginning of a video and are called "Pre-roll ads" Each time any viewer watches an ad all the way through (Complete advertisement without hitting the 'Skip Ad' option) or clicks on the ad the uploader of the video gets paid (Assuming he or she has fulfilled the two conditions required for monetization of the videos). There are other types of ad formats which we will discuss in later chapters.

So, the advertisers pay YouTube for being their advertisement partners, and YouTube in turn pays the YouTubers for uploading videos on their website. Any guesses on how much percentage of money out of the entire advertisement costs paid by the company, YouTube pays you? Well, YouTube pays straight 55% of the total money earned by playing ads. That means the maximum amount of money goes to the content creator. If you've heard people telling, YouTube barely pays peanuts, let me tell you it's a total MYTH! Let me also break the myth for you. YouTube pays fairly decent amount of its total earnings. Needless to say, that many traditional businesses don't promise such returns!

> *"YouTube pays straight 55% of the total money earned by playing ads. That means the maximum amount of money goes to the content creator."*

During the YouTube sessions I conduct, I've heard many people walking up to me and say "I've backed off from uploading my videos because I've heard people telling that YouTube only pays peanuts" I always help them in breaking this myth and going forward with uploading videos.

So, the next time you see someone saying that YouTube barely pays peanuts to the video uploaders and tries to de-motivate you from uploading videos, break the myth for them by telling the reality! Maximum amount of total earnings is paid to the content creator!

Now, how much is 55% depends on a lot of other conditions like the geographical location of the advertisers and the viewers of your videos, the brand image of the advertiser, type of ad displayed and so on. Let's not get into the analytics used by YouTube (Trust me, it's going to boggle up your minds)

Bottom line, this whole payment process is simple. The advertiser pays YouTube and YouTube in turn pays the YouTuber. Advertiser pays to YouTube by making use of the AdWords (that is purchasing the specific keywords at a specific price) And YouTube pays the YouTubers by making use of the AdSense.

So that was all about how YouTube works and how can you get paid as a YouTuber. Let's come to the eligibility criteria, years ago, YouTube policy were not very strict one could easily become a YouTube Partner and Monetize the videos, and thus even by uploading just one video, people were earning. When I started my YouTube channel A2C, this is how it was, the review process was being done by YouTube and my channel started earning money for me.

This gave way for a lot of fraudulent YouTubers who started uploading useless/ copyrighted content damaging the reputation of YouTube. Thus, YouTube made new rules and laid down some strict eligibility criteria, only on fulfillment of which, one can start earning money.

Until very recently, the eligibility criterion for monetization was to cross 10,000 views in total for the whole channel. But now, there's a small shock announced by Google on January 16, 2018. Here's the big shocking news: Google reported, "Once a YouTube channel reaches 4,000 watch hours in the previous 12 months and 1,000 subscribers it will be reviewed to join the YouTube Partner Program" In other words, all the channel creators now have to wait until 4,000 watch hours(watch hours concept explained in later chapters) are completed and obtaining 1,000 subscribers to enable monetization on their channel. Let me also tell you a surprising fact! Achieving this threshold limit won't be very hard because the number of YouTube Viewers and users has sky rocketed from the last 2 years. If you upload good content, know the right tips and tricks to increase the views on your channel (Only the Genuine tips and tricks) there's no stopping you from earning from your YouTube channel.

So, once you've fulfilled both the conditions of monetization, you'll start making money from your YouTube channel videos.

Read on the next chapter to know in detail about how Google AdSense works.

"Depend on the facts provided and not on what people say before you make the decision of uploading your videos!"

03. KNOWING GOOGLE ADSENSE PROGRAM

As I discussed in the last chapter, the program through which YouTube pays the YouTubers is called Google AdSense Program. For a beginner, knowing about the AdSense program is very important because that's how you'll be earning money. So, what exactly is Google AdSense?

Google AdSense is a Google owned application through which ads are shown in the websites or YouTube videos that participate in the Google AdSense program. As I told you, millions of companies around the world have partnered with YouTube for advertising their ads on the YouTube videos. So how does YouTube keep a track of how many viewers viewed the ads that were placed on your video? How do you, as the content creator or a YouTuber know about how much you're earning through your videos? Google AdSense is the answer to all these questions. It's a platform where video publishers in case of YouTube and website owners make money by placing ads on their website or YouTube videos.

For Websites/ Blogs - AdSense is nothing but an account that you need to open with Google using your gmail account and Google starts assigning you codes which you need to place on your blogs or websites. Where and how this placing of AdSense codes is to be done is a very technical and an elaborate topic which I wouldn't be sharing in this 'Beginners' Guide Book! When someone views the complete ad or clicks on the ad, you would earn money.

To earn from YouTube videos, we need to associate AdSense account with YouTube channel (Discussed in detail in later chapters) We can associate multiple channels with same AdSense account. For example, I have more than 2 channels and my wife has 2 channels too, but all the channels are associated to the same AdSense account. This helps to accumulate all the earnings into one account.

When I conduct my "YouTube for Beginners" sessions, many people ask me if they use the same Google AdSense account both for their website as well as their YouTube videos. I'd say absolutely YES! If you have both a website and a YouTube channel, it doesn't mean you need to have two different AdSense accounts. In fact, it's illegal to have more than 1 AdSense account for one person. You may have any number of Google IDs, but your Google AdSense account must remain one and must only be confined to one only for individual, for business you can apply for a new AdSense account! Remember the Golden rule: One person must have one, and only one Google AdSense account!

For example: I own a website by name receiveanswer.com which has blogs on how to build business, and many DIY ideas shared. I have one AdSense account with Google and I link the same AdSense account both on my website and my YouTube channel A2C. The total amount of money generated both by my videos and my website is clubbed together and deposited to my bank account which I've linked with the AdSense account. YouTube pays directly to the bank account linked to the Google AdSense account on the 21st of every month which gets credited to account in less than 7 days. But then there's a condition here. YouTube releases your payment only after you've crossed a bare minimum of 100 US Dollars. Only after you've crossed 10 US Dollars threshold, YouTube will enquire about the payment details and after the address validation, the process of payment gets simpler than ever! The money earned by you directly gets deposited to your bank account that's linked with your AdSense account.

> *"Remember the Golden rule: One person must have one, and only one Google AdSense account!"*

How to sign up for the Google AdSense Program?

Now that you've understood the basics of how Google AdSense works, let me tell you how to get your wheels started.

Step #1 - Create an AdSense account

The first step, of course, is to create the Google AdSense account by visiting the http://www.google.com/AdSense and creating your account there. The account through which you'll be logging in is the same that you use to log into your Gmail Account or YouTube.

Step #2 - Associating AdSense account to your YouTube channel

Login to your YouTube Channel navigate to YouTube Settings → View Additional Features → Under Channel click on Monetization → Click on Associate AdSense Account and follow the instructions on the screen.

Once done with this, Google takes some time to validate your channel. Until this validation is completed, the ads are not displayed by Google. Once their validation process is completed, you'll start earning according to the ads placed on your videos or website. This would usually take few days to sometimes a week or more.

Check the video in YouTube: How to link ADSENSE ACCOUNT To YouTube channel

Step #3 - Set up the payment details

The last and the final step is to set up your payment details. Only after you've crossed 10 US Dollars threshold, YouTube will provide an option on Google AdSense account to enter the payment details, ensure that the payment details provided by you are accurate.

Next for address validation Google would send an envelope to your postal address containing a code which you need to enter in AdSense account in order to start receiving money. Remember that you won't be receiving any payment until you've crossed the minimum threshold of 100 US Dollars. For example: If your previous month earning from YouTube is 80 US Dollars, then the payment would be made only in the next month once it crosses total of 100 US Dollars on the channel.

Well, that's all you need to know about Google AdSense Program as a beginner for YouTube.

04. WHO COULD PARTNER WITH YOUTUBE AND ELIGIBILITY CRITERIA?

N ow that you've learnt the basics of Google AdSense Program, the next step is to know about the eligibility criteria in order to partner with YouTube. Before that, for those of you who are wondering what 'Partnering with YouTube' means, let me brief you what it is. Being a partner with YouTube is nothing but you're monetizing your channel so that you can earn money from it. YouTube calls it partnering because they are sharing their revenue with you. Remember in the last chapter I mentioned that YouTube pays 55% of the total revenue generated to Youtubers or in other words YouTube partners. So, here's who can partner with YouTube.

Who can be a YouTube partner?
ANYONE!

Yes, you heard that right! Anyone can be a YouTube partner. There's no age bar to this nor it requires any specific qualification. Children who are younger than 18 years can also become YouTube partners. But, they have a small limitation here (If you call it so) YouTubers who are less than 18 years of age would be required to create a Google AdSense account in the name of their parents/guardians. Barring this limitation, there's no other age bars as to who could partner with YouTube. And anyone who wants to create and upload content can do so!

So, this explains many questions that are frequently asked in my "YouTube for Beginners" workshops like: (I've also provided answers to these questions in case you have same or similar questions)

We can see little children upload videos where they sing and dance, play with clay, balloons etc. How does it work for them? - Answer: There's no age bar to be a partner with YouTube.

Are these children earning too? - Answer: Well, the Google AdSense account to which the channel is linked earns, it could be parents or guardians (if the YouTube creator is under 18 years)

I'm 17 years old. Can I earn money from my YouTube channel? - Answer: Yes, you definitely can! You will or not depends on what content you're uploading and how many views your content is generating for your channel.

So now you know who can partner with YouTube. Read on to know how to generate views and the answer to the million-dollar question - What sort of content should I publish to make money while also pursuing something that you're passionate about! Trust me, that is the most important part of it!

05. THINGS TO CONSIDER BEFORE CREATING A YOUTUBE CHANNEL

It is never too late to start your own YouTube channel! The platform is on an all-time boom, and it is possible for you to begin from scratch and reach the pinnacles! However, there are a few things you must be considering if you wish to reap the best out of your efforts. The only thing that guarantees success in YouTube is perseverance, perseverance and perseverance! Persevere, but remember these things!

Be driven with inspiration!

If you want to start a YouTube channel, let the want be driven only with inspiration! Don't get into it because you can get famous or make money. Get into it with the inspiration of teaching the world something! You might be good at teaching DIY Crafts, cooking, you might want to talk about programming and app development, and so on. It could be anything, but there has to be something! Anything that can be done best is appreciation worthy and people laud for it! Be it something as simple as folding the cloths! Search it on YouTube and you'll be surprised!

Frequency of upload

Decide on how often you will be producing videos and uploading them. How long should the viewers wait before you can serve them another of your videos? While deciding, make sure you are being realistic and not overly enthusiastic without a point! The frequency matters in the long run, and if you fail to maintain your frequency, people might bounce away and unsubscribe!

Promotional strategies

If you think you will just upload videos and people will readily watch your videos, let me tell you that it won't happen in the beginning. You may go creating new videos for one whole year and still not garner awe inspiring numbers! At least in the initial stages, you have to promote your videos, and you should know the clear line between self-promotion and spamming!

Make sure your promotional strategies are in place. I am not saying you got to have a clear blueprint. Just using social media to its optimum capacity must just do fine!

06. HOW TO CREATE A YOUTUBE CHANNEL

Now that I have mentioned a few things you have to keep in mind, let me now tell you how to begin with your YouTube channel.

1. Firstly, log into YouTube with your Gmail account credentials

2. Your Gmail account is in itself a YouTube channel with your username same as the Gmail username

3. Unless you wish to brand yourself as the YouTube channel's name, choose to create a new channel (Creator Studio → My channel → Add New Brand/channel). I personally prefer creating a new channel, so that you can change the name of the channel later, if needed.

4. Name the channel as per your ideas, and you are ready to go!

But, how do you choose a suitable name for your channel? Should you just go with whatever strikes you, or should you try and optimize the name? Well, let me tell you how I chose my name. My channel is all about DIY crafts. First, I thought I'd name it Arts & Crafts. But very soon I realized the name is very generic. So, I abbreviated Arts and Crafts to A2C. The channel's name now is A2C Arts & Crafts. Now, even if someone just types A2C, my channel's name is suggested.

The reason I told you is that while you may have a name in mind, see how you can make it unique so that it doesn't get lost among generic names. While the name can be relevant to what your channel does, the uniqueness of the name will set it apart. If you want to Brand your own name as a channel, then you can very well go ahead! Also, before creating the channel name, search in YouTube if that name already exists. If yes, you must look for a different channel name.

07. WHAT VIDEOS CAN YOU MAKE TO PUBLISH ON YOUTUBE?

One of the most frequently asked questions in my 'YouTube for Beginners' session is "What sort of videos should I make to publish on YouTube?" In my entire session, this topic, I can say, steals the spotlight. Because at the end of the day, what content goes on your channel is the most important thing which is going to make you an YouTube star or just one among many YouTubers struggling to cross more than 1,000 subscribers. Before you start your channel, this is the most important question that you need to answer. Posting random content on any random subject at inconsistent times is of no use and it not only damages the reputation of your YouTube channel but will not help a bit in having engaged audience for your channel. So, let me answer the million-dollar question - *What* videos should I make to publish on YouTube?

PASSION FIRST

The very first suggestion I provide to people who ask me what videos must be made is to start a channel about something that you really are passionate about! It doesn't end there. You got to upload such videos in which you are showcasing your talent. Doing something which really interests you pays you off and it wouldn't even be difficult for you to do. Because we all love to do what we love to do, right? It's that simple!

The next question that could pop up in your mind now is "How do I know what really interests me?" Well, most people aren't clear on what exactly interests them. There are some people who are interested in almost everything like singing, painting, arts, cooking, dancing, fashion designing and then there are some who do not have special interest in anything. (Or they at least think so!) I'll give you a small hack here. The best way to know about the field in which you're really good at is by thinking about what talent of yours is most appreciated by your friends! Go back to your school days or college days. Recollect what was that special talent in you which was most appreciated and celebrated by your friends or professors? Well, *that* is your first best talent (Well, I have to say 'First' best talent because there are many people who are multi-talented) Investing little time in this talent can certainly help you to improve in that field.

Real Passion V/S Pseudo Passion

As I already told you, it's always best for you if you can start a channel showcasing your talent that you're extremely passionate about! Now, there are two types of passion. The first one is the real passion where you know that you really enjoy doing something and this opinion won't change from time to time. For example: Once a lover of music, always a lover of music! The second one is the Pseudo passion, which, as the name suggests is Pseudo or False. This opinion keeps fluctuating and it's not something you love doing with all your heart and soul. It's something you *think* you enjoy doing but in actuality, you aren't! For example: When you're humming a recent hit music, you may think you're loving it and that you really are passionate about music but then you don't sing the song for the next one month! This is Pseudo Passion which doesn't stay permanent and keeps fluttering every now and then with the change in trends, change in friend's tastes and other external factors. You need to understand the differences between Real Passion and Pseudo Passion and take a call only after you're sure about what your *Real* Passion is!

Why is it best to make videos about something you're passionate about?

Why should you make videos about something you really love? Why can't you just upload anything that's trending? Why can't you just do different things at different times on your channel? - These are certain questions that could pop up in your mind. Well, I'll tell you why.

1. Making videos that doesn't interest you might seem easy to make initially. But with time, you'll feel bored to make such videos

because you know it's not your passion and eventually you'll stop making videos. What follows next? All the followers or the views you got would all go down the drain as you stopped uploading videos.

2. You can never put your heart and soul into it. If it's not your passion, you will never be able to give your best! It'd become a 'Task' for you and you'll eventually lose all the interest you had while making your first video.

3. People cannot connect with you. Can you imagine Sachin Tendulkar making videos based on dance choreography? No right? Because his passion is cricket. We all have different interests and we're best at what we love and at what we think we're the best! People can't connect to you while you're doing something merely for the heck of making the video or by being impulsive that is clearly temporary. Thus, it'll leave you leading nowhere.

You can NOT stand the competition. It's a world of competition and people who are genuinely interested in the field will always have a upper hand over you because they're putting in genuine efforts! Your viewers will definitely know who's really passionate and who's just trying to make some random videos just to stay in the race? There have been YouTubers who've been washed away from YouTube because they couldn't sustain the competition their competitor posed!

These are the main reasons on why you should ALWAYS focus on making videos that really interests you (Unless you're looking at making only a bunch of 4 to 5 videos). If you're looking forward to creating a channel that has an engaged group of audience and be a YouTube sensation, you got to make videos which are your true interests!

SCOPE NEXT!

The first thing you need to consider is the passion factor. After you know about your passion, the second thing you need to consider is the scope of that passion to generate views for you. In other words, has your passion got the potential to grab the attention of the viewers? You need to weigh your passion with the scope it has got to generate views for you.

Let's say you're passionate about stamp collection and you've been doing it since years. You wish to make a video showcasing your collections. But can it be made into a channel that has the potential of uploading at least 25 videos? Has it got audience base? The best way to check this is by typing "Best stamp collections" on YouTube and looking at the number of views generated by not only the topmost video but also others that show up. This will give you a bare idea if your talent or interest has the potential of attracting audience's attention for not only one time, but consistently as and when you upload videos on your channel. Starting a channel about a subject that interests you but has no or very low audience engagement will only provide you personal satisfaction but NOT a strong YouTube community. And thus, I'd say it's not a great idea! Choose something that both interests you and has the potential of generating good audience base at the same time! It's a win-win deal then!

> *"Starting a channel about a subject that interests you but has no or very low audience engagement will only provide you personal satisfaction but NOT a strong YouTube community."*

What to do when there's a conflict between 2 talents? (For those of you who are gifted with Multi-talented personality)

There can be chances where you feel that there's a conflict between two of your interests. Two interests are equally loved by you and your friends, you're talented in both of them. What can you do then? The solution is simple! Pick the one that has got a stronger audience engagement on YouTube. Put in other words, go for the one that has good audience base of the two!

For example: Let's say you're talented and are equally passionate about both cooking and reviewing cosmetic products. Look at the audience base that's available for both these categories by simply searching these on YouTube. You'll be able to see the number of views cooking videos get and the number of views reviews about cosmetic products get! Weigh both of them and take your call! This way, the conflict between 2 interests or talents can be bridged.

Once your 1st channel starts generating consistent views and has good subscribers, you can think of starting a new channel with other things you are passionate about.

Remember that there's always scope for trial and errors

You can be talented in more than one skill! You can get confused about which is your true passion but it's Okay! As long as you're trying hard to discover what you're truly amazing at, it's absolutely okay! It might take you some time understand your true passion. So, does that mean you don't start making videos at all and spend time thinking about what your actual passion is? Waiting for the "Golden Realization Time!"? The answer is NO. You don't need to wait for the time when you can be 100% sure about your true talent. There's always scope for trial and errors. It's totally okay to make mistakes! Learn from your mistakes and move on. *But remember clearly, what mistakes can be done and what should not be done. We will talk about that in detail in upcoming chapters.*

In my own personal experience, I've experimented a lot before I actually discovered what was my true passion was and what was working out for me. (The scope factor) I first started off by exposing my painting skills. I was great at it back in school days, but I'd lost the hang of it when I started it. I took time to try and improve but the audience response wasn't really encouraging for me. What I started for showing my pencil sketching and painting skills slowly turned into the channel where I taught people different types of Origami paper folding. Only after the Origami paper folding did I actually get into doing what I'm doing at present - Arts and Crafts with mostly electrical gadgets! So, it took me a lot of time (almost 6 months) and trials and errors before I learnt what worked out the best for me! So, don't back out if you fail once, try again with a new concept and eventually you'll know what works out the best for you! Remember that no one can become a star in one day; give yourself some time to explore the star in you! Once you've explored it, there's no stopping you from shining!

"Remember that no one can become a star in one day; give yourself some time to explore the star in you!"

O8. THINGS TO CONSIDER BEFORE YOUR FIRST VIDEO!

We have already discussed what videos you can make and how to begin with your YouTube channel. Now is your turn. It is time you consider three important things before embarking on your YouTube journey!

Every successful YouTuber shares three main ingredients based on motivation; Target audience, topic coverage and the purpose of the channel!

Target audience is WHO you want your videos to reach to!

There is audience for all content. But which kind of audience you are targeting? The target audience could be decided on many terms. It could be according to the age group, geography, taste for art and so on. For instance, are you targeting school kids and want to make something for them? Make yourself clear on who is it you want to cater to!

Your topic coverage is basically WHAT your videos are going to be about!

Now that you know who your target audience is, decide what you wish to do for them. It needn't necessarily be in this order. You can always choose what kind of videos you want to do and then see who your target audience for that niche are. The choice is yours but the clarity on both of these is a must!

Purpose of the channel is WHY your videos must be watched!

Yeah, you have a YouTube channel, you have a niche of videos and you have certain target audience for that. But why should they watch your video out of many videos that may possibly serve content on the same niche? That is the purpose you give them. You need to give them a purpose to choose your video! As simple as that!

Say for example, in A2C channel I give my best to keep the creativity as simple as possible so that anyone can do it on their own, that's my purpose.

These three things matter a lot when you launch your YouTube channel to be one of the successful YouTube channel.

09. ENTERTAINMENT V/S VALUE ADDITION OF A YOUTUBE CHANNEL

After deciding to start a YouTube channel, one of the first questions that anyone would stumble upon is "Should my channel have value additions to the audience or is it okay if it's just entertaining?" This is also one of the frequently asked questions in my YouTube workshops. Well, if you look at the channels that are performing really great with millions of subscribers, you'll notice that the Channel genre fall either into the entertainment category or the value addition one!

You can check it out yourself. Check for the channels that are based on personality development, communication skills and so on and you will see millions of subscribers to these channels. Similarly, check out a singing YouTube sensation channel or a team of skilled people performing a specific art, you'll still find many subscribers to the channel. Pick a totally entertainment-based channels like stand-up comedies and you won't be surprised to see millions of views and subscribers again here!

So, what does that say? What can we conclude? Which is the most trending niche? Should your channel have value addition to the viewer or just entertain them? The answer is - It doesn't matter! Yes, you heard that right! It doesn't matter at all if your channel is entertaining the audience or providing them value additions, as long as your content is creative and interesting, you will have audience for your channel. Think about it. Out of billion users, there will be audience for all types of niches! So, I always say that just do what you're best at Put in your best efforts at whatever you're good at and the world will follow you. (In its literal sense as well.... I mean people will support you by subscribing to your channel)

"It doesn't matter at all if your channel is entertaining the audience or providing them value additions, as long as your content is creative and interesting, you will have audience for your channel."

While some use YouTube for entertainment, some use it for learning and adding value to their lives! Most of us use it for both purposes! Hence there will be audience for all types of niches! Just figure out what you're best at and let the world know about it!

10. WHY SHOULD PEOPLE WATCH YOUR VIDEO?

Whether you are making videos about fashion tips, cooking recipes, car reviews, film reviews, simple DIYs, music videos, travel tips or anything, chances are good that you are not the only one! There's always someone else who's doing whatever you're doing! With so many competitors who are giving out the same content that you are, why should people watch your video? This is the fundamental question you need to ask yourself! So, how do you add more value to your videos? Simply put, what makes *your* channel stand out from the lot?

If you look at the channels with highest number of views and subscribers, you'll see a common trend. All these channels have a special element that makes them the best in their own niche! They're doing something extra over and above than what their competitors are doing! This little 'extra' scoop to their channel is what that's going to make a world of difference to the viewers! So what's your channel's 'extra' scoop? If you don't have anything that's extra ordinary in your channel, you can't expect your channel to be extra ordinary!

Let me tell you some tips on how you can add that 'extra' scoop to your channel. Mind you that these tips are just to give you a broader perspective and open you to more ideas and are not 'Go-to' rules! These are tips that have worked out for many successful channels! Taking inspiration from these tips can help you discover or create a special element to your channel!

"If you don't have anything that's extra ordinary in your channel, you can't expect

How to make your channel stand out?

Number 1 - Reflect YOUR personality in your channel

People are not just watching your videos for the information you're providing or just for your content! They're mainly hunting for a different perspective! You need to add a personal touch to your videos which should reflect your own personality! For example: If you make travel videos by adding a humor touch simply because you're personally a fun lover, the audience that likes the funny style will become your loyal audience! There can be hundred other travel videos, but your audience will only watch your channel because they like the element of 'comedy' in travel videos. This was just an example. Reflect your personality in your channel and your type of audience will have great interest in your channel. That's how your channel can stand out from your competitors.

Number 2 - Differentiate your content from similar content

In order to stand out, you need to do something that's different from what others are doing. Browse through the videos that are uploaded by others on similar content and note down the common things. Now, you must be doing something that's beyond what these people are adding. Differentiate your content from that of theirs. For example: Let's say you're uploading cooking videos. While all others are teaching how the recipe is done, why don't you tell what the best occasions or times to serve these recipes are? Or maybe tell the health benefits of these recipes? Or add a little bit of story on how you stumbled upon this recipe? And so on.... There can be plenty ways of differentiating your content. Discover what works best for you and incorporate those in your channel.

Number 3 - Upload seasonal content

Whatever niche you may be in, according to "What's trending around the world", learn how you can tailor your channel making it relatable to such trending events or sensations. In my own personal experience, this has worked out a lot for me. There was a time when fidget spinners were a hot trending object and people were going bonkers over this gadget. I made three videos about fidget spinners:

- How to make fidget spinners - with nuts
- How to make fidget spinners - with bearings
- How to make fidget spinners - without bearings

Since it was a trending search, people who weren't my subscribers viewed it too and they probably even subscribed to my channel! A similar thing happened when the song "Despacito" by Luis Fonsi became viral! Many YouTube music channels replicated Despacito in all different languages and versions! So, keep an eye out for something that's going viral and try to relate to your channel! It's always a good value addition for your channel. (Needless to say, it must be kept relevant. I couldn't have done anything with Despacito because it was irrelevant to my channel whose main focus is on arts and crafts)

Number 4 - Great videos must have great video titles!

The videos that are uploaded by you must have appropriate video titles that'll grab the attention of your viewers! If you're able to find a suitable title that's both catchy and at the same relevant to what your video is all about, it's the best thing for your channel to get maximum views. After making your video, think of at least 4 to 5 titles and finalize the one that's both catchy to the viewers as well as relevant.

Example: If you want to show the recipe of French Fries, instead of using, "How to make French fries" as the video title, you could use, "Homemade Crispy French Fries Recipe" which suggests that the recipe is homemade and also crispy.

Number 5 - Passion pays off!

Whatever be the video you're making and uploading, ensure that you're really passionate about it. Because passion is like the glaring spark that adds an element of elegance to your videos, which we discussed a lot in previous chapter. For example: I'm not the best person to upload reviews about cars because I'm not so passionate about different sports cars! So, if I choose to upload such videos, people will not find it special thus my channel will be a doom! Reflecting your passion in your videos will really pay you off! Between someone who's making videos with amazing technical brilliance and the best editing and the one who's made a video with full of enthusiasm and passion, the video with passion always stands out!!!

So that was a small brief on how you can make your channel stand out.

As I already told you, mind that these are some tips that have worked for me and many other successful channels and you must discover or create a special factor for your own channel that's totally unique! Because the world loves what's original and unique! Add the 'extra' scoop and you'll definitely stand different from your competitors!

My final words on building a genuine audience base – Serve your audience! In other terms, provide content that adds a value proposition to your audience, money would follow automatically! But on the other hand, if your focus is only on money, you may end up with neither money nor a good audience base!

> *"Provide content that adds a value proposition to your audience, money would follow automatically! But on the other hand, If your focus is only on money, you may end up with neither money nor a good audience base!"*

11. DO'S AND DON'TS ON YOUR YOUTUBE CHANNEL

After making up your mind on starting a new YouTube channel, the next step before actually starting the channel is knowing what can or should be done and what cannot or shouldn't be done. This will not only save a lot of your time, which in other case would be wasted doing the trial and error methods, but also adds good quality to your overall channel. Knowing these do's and don'ts will help a lot in future. I must say that I wish someone had told me all these before I started my YouTube channel because I did invest a lot of time in exploring and learning all by myself through experiences (Good ones and...the bad ones too) As the proverb says, "A wise man learns from the mistakes of others" learning what should not be done by looking at the mistakes done by others is a wise thing to do! So, let's start with the Don'ts first.

What you should NOT DO on your YouTube channel

(This is the most crucial thing. Read it carefully as violation of these may lead to ban of your channel by YouTube.)

1. Posting Nudity or sexual content

Nudity or sexual content is strictly forbidden on the YouTube. If the content shows nudity or any sort of sexual content, your channel can be banned by YouTube forever and you may not be allowed to start that channel ever again. Although your niche is something very different from nudity or sexual content and you've posted it just a couple of times, it is still considered as a strict violation of the YouTube policies. So nudity and sexual content is a big NO.

2. Harmful or dangerous content

Videos that show violence directly or indirectly by just teaching how to use harmful and dangerous weapons are considered as a violation of the YouTube policies which amount to removal of all the content from your channel.

3. Violent or graphic content

Just like the harmful or dangerous content, any sort of violent and graphic content that creates disturbance in the mind is also considered as violation of the YouTube policies.

4. Posting content without having the copyrights required to post it

If you post content and use any backgrounds, music or text without having the legal copyrights in using it, your channel could be banned by YouTube. There are YouTube video auditing authorities who keep an eye on content creators violating the copyright issues. And then there are also cases where the true owner of a copyrighted content writes a complaint letter to YouTube, which shall again lead to adverse consequences for your channel. There's a detailed chapter on what happens when you violate the copyright policies and its consequences which can be referred for more information.

5. Hateful content

Publishing hateful content against any person, community, part, religion, country is a clear violation of the YouTube policies laid down. This again leads to taking down your channel with all the previous content posted by YouTube. (P.S.: Don't tell who you hate and why you hate someone on any social media platforms for your own good)

6. Threats

Some people who do not stop at posting hateful content move on to provide threats through videos. This has very serious consequences along with removal of your channel from YouTube.

7. Spam, misleading metadata, and scams

Misleading metadata is used by some channels just so that they get more people to watch their videos. There can also be misleading thumbnails which clearly deceives the users and is considered a corrupt practice. Scam videos wherein the content creator is misleading the audience just for getting more clicks is also considered to be against the YouTube policies.

8. Songs or pieces of music that aren't eligible for revenue sharing

Using music for your channel while you're showing something to your viewers is a great practice. But using those music or parts of music that aren't eligible for revenue sharing amounts to violation of the YouTube policies. You can refer to the detailed chapter explaining about the 'Copyrights violations and its consequences' for more knowledge in this regard.

9. Using Music, Graphics and pictures, Movie or TV visuals without explicit permission from the content owner.

Suppose your competitor has used very powerful music and graphics on his or her channel and you're wishing to use it to for your own channel. So, what do you do? Simple! Just use the same music and graphics or just copy it! Is that so? No! Not at all! If you wish to use any music, graphics and pictures, TV visuals etc. that's created by some other person on YouTube, you are eligible to use it on your channel only if you obtain the explicit approval from the content creator. Using unethical methods to copy what's been done by others will lead to serious consequences and surely the existence of your channel on YouTube would go on a toss.

These are some DO NOTS on your YouTube channel that are strictly prohibited from being done by the YouTube. To know the entire list of Don'ts on YouTube refer to the YouTube community guidelines. Remember that violations can not only have serious consequences but might also lead to removal of all your content on your channel by YouTube. They are called DO NOTS for a reason and if you want to make it big on YouTube, you need to stick only to the ethical ways!

> *"Remember that violations can not only have serious consequences but might also lead to removal of all your content on your channel by YouTube. They are called DO NOTS for a reason and if you want to make it big on YouTube, you need to stick only to the ethical ways!"*

What you SHOULD DO on your YouTube channel

This book has talked about what you should do in many parts of different chapters and, so I'm only listing down what should be done on YouTube. There are separate detailed chapters on most of the areas mentioned below. In different chapters, I've told you How to do what's to be done on YouTube! Let's run through what are the DOs on YouTube

1. Create engaging and interesting content

2. Engage with your audience

3. Have Call-To-Action at the end of your video

4. Have a great ending to your videos to leave a lasting impression in the minds of the people who watch your videos

5. Improve the quality of your videos with time

6. Learn the best editing skills to make your videos professional day by day

7. Have attractive thumbnails to your videos that'll catch the attention of your viewers

8. Have suitable metadata, title and description of the videos with relevant as well as catchy content

9. Work towards increasing the watch time of your channel

10. Create playlists to add-on to the watch time of your channel

11. Do not delay in getting the first 100 subscribers to your channel. It's possible and can be done on the very first day of starting your channel.

12. Strive on getting more and more subscribers for your channel

13. Make some collaborations with other YouTube channel owners wherever it's relevant in doing so

14. Promote your videos across various social media platforms to get the maximum exposure and the wide audience

15. ASK the viewers to subscribe to your channel and have no hitch in doing so

That's just a glimpse of what you should be doing on your channel. Turn the pages of all other chapters to learn *'How'* to do the aforesaid DOs on your YouTube channel.

12. CONSEQUENCE OF NOT FOLLOWING YOUTUBE GUIDELINES

I have chosen to talk to you about it in the very beginning because I would not want you to go through what my brother (who also owns a YouTube channel) did. If you violate guidelines of YouTube, there will be high risks at stake! I will take you through a few things that you should strictly not do, and I will explain it with personal references, so you understand that the YouTube Guidelines stand for what they speak!

No Copyright strikes!

Don't use copyrighted content, strictly! It's a big NO! If you use a copyrighted image, a video clip or music without explicit permission, there are extremely high chances that your channel gets a strike. Three strikes on your channel and the channel will face existential crises!

I had searched for free music on google and used that in coupe of my videos, unfortunately after few months I got copyright strike on 2 videos. Anyone can upload music on many websites, at times we don't know who is the actual copyright owner, so don't just believe what they call as "Free Music" on the internet. YouTube has its own Audio Library from which one can take music's which allow monetization.

Also, my brother was so eager to get more and more views that he once compiled a video, using clips of Super bikes. His channel did get strikes for that! The story doesn't end there!

Don't watch your own video repeatedly and click on Ads yourselves!

Again, my brother didn't stop there. He was overly excited about earning from his channel. He watches his own videos repeatedly and clicked on the Ads that showed up so that he earned soon! Obviously, YouTube algorithms are very smart, and they totally banned his YouTube channel once and for all!

However, my brother wrote a letter to YouTube and after 6 months, he got his channel up and running, along with strict warning.

Do you think the agony ended there?

No spams and misleading tags!

After some months, while my brother was doing great on YouTube, earning good income every month, his channel got blocked all of a sudden again. This time, he clearly hadn't used any copyrighted material and he hadn't even made the mistake of clicking on the ads himself. He lost his cool and even complained to the Cyber police on how YouTube blocked his channel unnecessarily. That is when we learnt that this time, he had used misleading tags in his videos which are considered spamming. And since he was a repeated offender, YouTube had blocked him again. Let me explain what misleading tags are. For instance, if you have a Car review of Swift Dzire, your tags must be Maruthi, Maruthi Swift Dzire review and so on, and it shouldn't be Rolls Royce, Ferrari and the like. If you try to mislead YouTube with the irrelevant tags, YouTube will spam you! So, don't ever use irrelevant misleading tags for your videos!

Well, these are some things that I have practically seen myself. So, I strongly advise you against these practices. But if you feel the need of using copyrighted material, it is wise to get explicit permission from the copyright owner. You just have to write an e-mail seeking permission to use their content so that they don't strike your channel in the future! I guess that's about it. For detailed Guidelines, **I suggest you go through the entire YouTube Community guidelines before starting out.**

13. VERIFYING YOUR YOUTUBE ACCOUNT

Verifying your YouTube channel gives you added benefits to you while uploading, such as removing the time limit of 15 minutes, live streaming, ability to add external website links in End Screens and YouTube cards and even allows you to customize your video thumbnails. The verification process can be completed either with a voice call or a text message. Regardless of what you choose, you will be given a six-digit code which you must enter on the verification page. What I have observed is, though the process takes just a few minutes, a lot of YouTube channel owners remain unaware about this, missing out on the extra benefits that the verified accounts pack with them!

In a few steps, I will guide you how to easily verify your YouTube account. Read on!

1. Access your YouTube channel through your web browser, the option will be placed next to your channel name. Click on YouTube Setting → Status and Features then click on Verify.

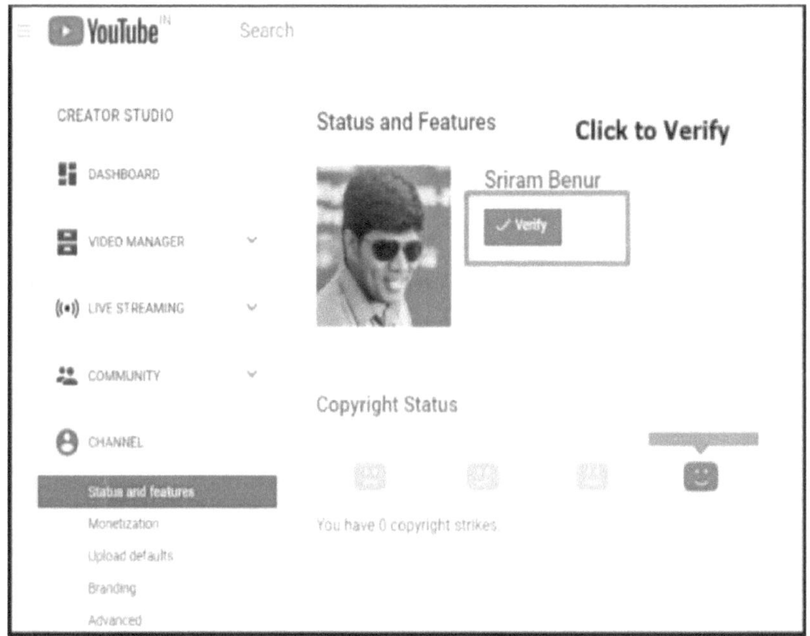

2. Once you click on it, you will be sent to the page where you must be selecting your method of verification and the country. Make sure you have signed in for this.

3. Choose the country you belong to in the drop-down box.

4. Choose your option of getting the verification code. It could either be a voice call or a text message. A few countries might not be allowed to receive messages sent from Google, so you may have to choose verifying through voice calls, if you belong to such country.

5. Just type in your phone number

6. Once you click on 'Submit' you will receive the verification code through the means that you have selected. You must wait for a minute or two to receive a text or a call. If you don't receive the code within fair amount of time, you must be requesting a new one. Remember that only two YouTube accounts can be verified through one phone number in a year, exceeding which you will receive error message.

7. Type in the six-digit code for verification and click 'Submit'. You will receive a message showing that you have successfully verified

your YouTube account.

Well, now that your account is verified, you will gain access to the features that I earlier told you about. Here is how you can go through all of them.

1. Access the Features Page through your web browser. You will be sent to the page which shows the different privileges your account has access to. What showed 'Ineligible' earlier would be showing 'Not Enabled' which you must manually Enable and some features would have automatically Enabled after you have verified your account. The status of verification will also be displayed under the username.

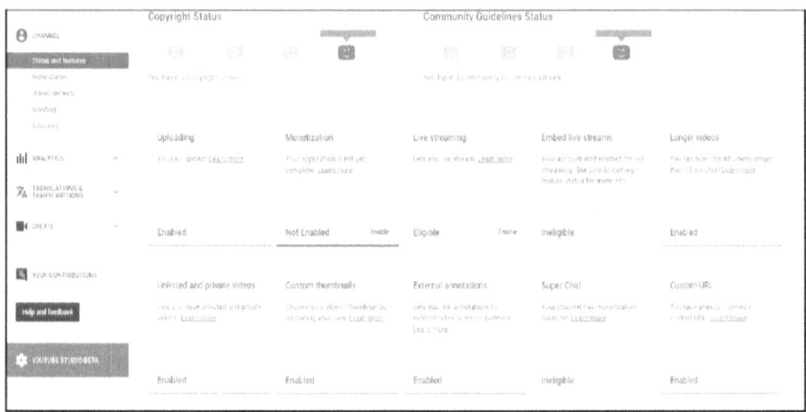

2. The status of your ratings will be shown under your username. These are the ratings for Community/copyright guidelines. Three infractions on your channel may decrease your ratings as a consequence of which you would lose out on a few benefits, based on how grave the violation is. If you see a smiley face green status, it means your account is safe.

3. Learn more about End Screens and YouTube cards here. These can be added in your videos to give links and information. I will be discussing more about the power this feature has later on.

4. Check the feature of custom thumbnails. A thumbnail is an image preview which will be shown on the listing of videos. Once you have verified, you will be allowed to customize these thumbnails

while you are uploading, and even add thumbnails to the videos that already exist.

5. Though the verification process would have allowed you to access the feature of Live streaming, you must still turn on this feature on the Features page. You just have to click enable under the Live streaming column.

With that, I guess you would have completed a tiny yet a vital procedure in your YouTube account. It's time we move on to the next chapter!

14. HOW DO YOU UPLOAD VIDEOS TO YOUTUBE THE RIGHT WAY?

In this chapter, I wish to talk about a strategy which is highly important, and something that would not just save five minutes of your time for every video that you upload, but will also ensure that you get more traffic for all your YouTube videos without any extra work!

If you've been observing, I take discerned look at each setting and feature that YouTube has to offer because each of such features or settings has the potential to bring a lot of traffic to your videos if you learn how to use it!

YouTube default uploading settings

Default settings are a way to semi-automate the uploading process as well as optimize videos.

While having specific descriptions as well as tags for individual videos can bring you good traffic, having a generalized tags for all of your videos will only ensure more traffic. And this is what the default settings will offer you! This feature will not just allow you to have settings that are fixed in prior for each video you upload, but will also allow you to change them for individual videos. Don't you think it would be amazing if you saved up to half an hour for every ten videos that you upload?

Finding the Default settings page

Click on YouTube Settings → View additional features → from the left-hand side links select Upload Defaults.

If not for people who aren't even aware that the Video uploading default settings exist, most of them don't know how they can use default settings other than using it for optimizing the uploading process. But rarely will you find people talking about using this feature for getting high traffic! First, I will share with you about how to configure the default settings and then talk about how you can use it for a higher purpose as obtaining more traffic!

- Once you get to the defaults section, check out the things that you need to fill in, and take your time to decide what should go into those!
- Choose your privacy level based on your preference
- Select the categories that your videos fit into, and make sure you don't do it irrelevantly
- Fill in Default title, description tags which will stay common for all videos. You can override these settings for individuals as well
- Selecting the checkbox for Monetization will ensure that your videos are monetized automatically once uploaded.
- Select the needed Ad formats, I would prefer to select all of them along with Ad breaks

Select other options as per your preference. Now that you know how you should set your defaults, it is time you understood how to optimize it not to just save time but get more viewership!

Absorb the details

Do you wish to use the Default settings feature for more than just optimizing video uploading process? Then you must keep your eyes open to fine details. The most antique method of getting your video to the first page was to acquire huge number of links. But these days, obtaining traffic is more about brand recognition and social interaction.

Ranking the videos through Default tags!

Higher the number of mentions of your brand and higher the frequency of interaction from your viewers, higher the priority you get to enjoy! The moment you have a video that is performing good by getting certain number of views per day, and people are interacting with the video (interact as in watch time is more, like it, comment on it and add it to their favorites), you will get some brand recognition.

And the best part is you can replicate the power of this particular video to other of your videos as well. All by just using the brand tags in your videos!

This is where YouTube default settings help you because you tend to forget including your Brand name (name of your channel or business) along with intensely researched tags that will summarize the idea of your entire channel example for A2C Arts And Crafts generic tags could be crafts, best out of waste, School Projects, homemade craft etc. You can call it Power tags since they act like a connecting wire between all your videos, and I have clearly noticed videos with such tags always show up high in the search rankings!

Use the Power Of Social Proof!

Another technique you can use which works on a psychological level than just organic traffic or SEO is to utilize the Default settings to display the usernames and links of your Social media profiles since those who will like your content will be interested in following you as well.

Stay relevant to those top 10 videos that are performing great in your niche. You can use them as your best examples, and take inspiration from their titles and descriptions!

Settings up the Default description is a one-time work but you should ensure that you display all your social media profiles such as Facebook pages, Twitter profiles, Google Community pages, Blogposts and so on! This will create some conversation around your brand.

15. OPTIMIZING THE TITLE, DESCRIPTION AND TAGS FOR YOUR VIDEOS

Technically speaking, you'd have started the process of optimizing your videos way before your video goes into the production. The real success on YouTube lies in the production value and the content! It doesn't matter where your video would stand on the search list since there is always space for improvements.

Once the video is uploaded and made public, there are two major ways that would help your video to be unique from the lot!

1) A title that is click-worthy

2) Description that is intriguing

Both these aspects must precisely depict the video's content in order to compel people to click on it and watch it fully. These two aspects give you the space to portray what value your video has got, and that is when people realize why they should be watching your video!

Zeroing in on a Title for your YouTube video

The very first criteria users seek for when they are searching a video is a title which is relevant, and which can provide the answer to what they are searching for. However, that is not necessarily the only purpose the title serves.

The title will also help YouTube in understanding what your video is all about, and when it must be showing up as a result of certain search. This is the reason why recognizing the relevant keywords and adding them to your video title is considered to be one among the best methods of optimizing your videos.

For instance, if your video is about making French fries at home, choosing a title like 'Cooking French fries' will not be very descriptive. Instead, if you choose a title like 'How to make crispy French fries at home?' there are greater chances of your video showing up on the top. Always remember that your video title must be descriptive and keyword rich!

Pandering to the ranking system of YouTube as well as the potential viewers become equally imperative, and thus, you should choose to come up with a title which can accomplish both these goals. Though you have about 100 characters to play with, concentrate on depicting your video's value concisely and try to keep your titles within 70 characters (including spaces)!

Having said that, you must also ensure your video actually has relevance to the keywords you are targeting. If not, YouTube will come to a conclusion that you are using misleading tags.

Developing a great video title can be an act of balance, but with poise, you can pull it off!

Writing the description

With the description of your video, you will have some more space to experiment with. I have noticed people taking full advantage of the maximum character limit (5000). But I've seldom seen these people using the space wisely. You may have observed that most descriptions will have a URL in the first line or some links in the initial sentences. But one should understand that when users are on YouTube, they aren't searching for links the way they do on Google. What they are looking for is videos with answers, and descriptions that will help them decide if the video is worth watching entirely so they can find their answers.

While the video is watched, under the video's title, you will have under 300 characters to tell people about the relevance and the value of your content, and filling it with links may not be a good option. Besides, starting the description of a video with a URL could essentially tamper your video's search rankings by decreasing the CTR (Click Through Rates) from search, and this is not a good signal for ranking!

What I suggest is that you briefly explain what your video is about in the above 300characters, and later use optimal the maximum character limit you are provided with. Considering the example of the French fries, you could write the entire recipe of making French fries, and that would act like a blog in itself! When you write blog like description, you are enriching your video description with relevant keywords, and thereby enriching your Metadata!

Optimizing the Video Tags!

While the above two aspects that help your video stand out from the crowd, your video tags are what will take your video into the crowd in the first place! Tags are a very crucial aspect of your video since they help your videos show up on relevant search results. Choosing the right tags will help your videos show up as 'Suggested Videos' as well! So, how do you choose the right tags?

There are three variants for these tags, and I will explain them to you with an example. Suppose you are making a video review of smartphone 'Samsung S8':

- **Specific tags/Effective tags** – Samsung, Samsung S8, smartphone

- **Compound tags** - Review of the new Smartphone S8, how is Samsung S8 Smartphone, Samsung S8 smartphone review

- **Generic tags** – Reviews, Electronic gadgets, Weekly review of Smartphones, Electronic gadgets reviews

I hope you understood the idea behind these tags with these examples. Let me summarize it. With specific tags, you will specifically use the keywords that users are specifically searching for! With compound tags, you are writing sentences which users would possibly use to find what they are looking for. And with generic tags, you are making your videos relevant to other similar videos so that if someone is watching a review of some other phone, your review of Samsung S8 too shows up!

There is something called as misspelled tags as well. For instance, if you have a video wherein you teach kids 'How to make paper Aeroplane', you might as well consider adding tags like 'How to make paper Aroplanes'. The idea behind is to predict the common spelling errors and adding them as your tags so that even if the user is typing a misspelled word, your video shows up because it is relevant to what they were trying to search for!

Well, that was an elaborate explanation of how you must be optimizing your video titles, descriptions and tags. But remember, the smartest video titles, descriptions and tags wouldn't mean anything if your video lacks value. Your video content is the protagonist while these things are its sidekicks! Ensure your protagonist impresses the audience!

16. YOUTUBE CHANNEL BRANDING

Your YouTube channel is like a storefront! Gift it the perfect look that would flaunt your style, and make sure you brand it like a pro!

When I say brand here, I mean the literal Branding - the usage of icons, banners, thumbnails and so on! This will give your channel the right look. So, how can one create a sensational look with their Branding?

Content is important - The brand designs must be relevant to the kind of content you generate. You would certainly wish the Brand conveys what your viewers can anticipate to see.

It must be familiar - The Brand design you choose must depict the style of your channel in a consistent and logical manner. It must convey the channel's core message to the viewers so they know what they are getting into. You can just keep it simple. Ensure all your videos, including the channel trailer correspond to your Branding.

Must be easy to find - The Brand designs of your channel should make it seamless for the channel visitors to search and find your channel. When tagged using metadata right, and posting your videos on the right social media platforms, your channel brand design will help your viewers in recognizing your channel easily.

The Channel Icon

Your channel icon will be the face of your YouTube channel everywhere across YouTube and Google, you can see this image in the top right corner of the page when you're logged into YouTube. Ensure that the icon looks great both small and large. It will also appear on the left-hand side of your YouTube banner as an overlay, and also on watch page. It could also be displayed on the right-hand side of other channels' pages if you've been chosen as one among their featured YouTube channels.

First, you should ensure your icon is either a rounded picture or a square one which can render at 98×98 px.

The best image you upload must be an 800×800 picture in either BMP, PNG or JPG formats!

Channel Art

This one is the banner right at the top of the channel page. This is a great place to showcase the personality of your channel. Also, the channel art appears on every platform where the visitors watch your channel, be it TV, tablets or Mobile phones.

Make sure you upload a picture of resolution 2560×1440 px.

Description of the Channel

The Channel Description will be displayed in the About tab which will give the viewers a brief overview of what could be expected of the channel. It also gets displayed when viewers hover above the channel icon on watch page. You can write up to 1000 characters and can also include links.

Your channel description must tell viewers what your channel is about. You can also consider mentioning the kind of content you would be producing, what your upload frequency would be and the like.

Custom Thumbnails

These are a really good way of packaging your video series with consistent feel and look. It would also help the visitors choose your video out of a plethora of thumbnails. Recently, a question came to me of a person who attended my seminar, asking how thumbnails would make a difference. I was prepared for this question since I was anyway going to explain the importance of thumbnails. I showed five packets of different colors but of same size, to the attendees. I asked them which packet would they choose. While a few chose yellow, some chose blue and so on. Once they were done choosing, I showed them that all the packets had the same Chocolate wrapped in different colors, nothing more!

The subtle learning here is that even if your content is at par with similar content, some might choose the latter just because they can! So, how do you grab their attention? By thumbnails!

Your thumbnail must flaunt the content that you have! A picture can speak a thousand words, so make your thumbnail talk! Choose a bright, bold as well as legible font for your thumbnails. You can also consider conducting separate photoshoots rather than taking a screenshot from the video that you've made!

Make them bright, bold and legible.

Watermark

This is a logo that is embedded on each of your YouTube videos, and you can enable them so they appear on the bottom right hand side corner of the videos. The Watermark will help you in promoting your brand all across the video. While watching on laptops and desktops, this watermark will even let your viewers subscribe to your YouTube channel without pausing the video or leaving it. Your viewers will be able to recognize that a certain video is from your channel the moment they take a look at the watermark.

In order to make the most out of your watermark, consider the kind of visual message you want to send out with your watermark. Do you wish to use the channel's logo or rather include an image which would invite the visitors to subscribe? Make your pick!

To set the watermark, click on YouTube settings → View Additional Features → and then Branding

Make sure to select Entire Video for Display time.

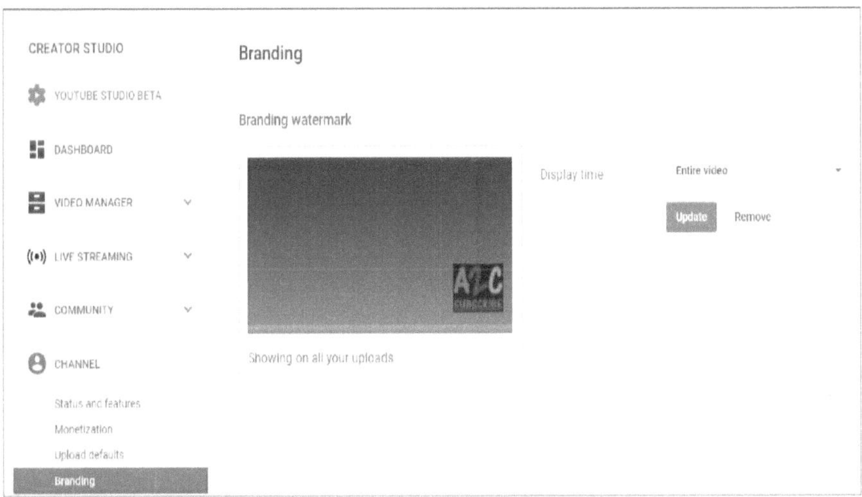

Channel Trailer

The moment someone opens your channel page, the first video that shows up is your Channel trailer, that is if you have it. This video should be less than 2 minutes. It will give an overview of what your channel is about. It would be the first thing the unsubscribed user sees when your channel page is opened. Hence, you need to ensure you make long lasting impression and compel these users to subscribe to your channel seeking for more!

To set the Channel Trailer navigate to Channel Home page → Click on Customize Channel → Click on For New Visitors you can set it from here

17. EDITING YOUR YOUTUBE VIDEOS

As important as it is to shoot the video well, the editing plays a vital role too. The post production is basically stitching multiple video shots into a persuasive, cohesive single video!

Earlier, post production was a time consuming and a costly process which asked for pricey professional tools. However, these days, you can edit the videos on your PCs with the help of low cost editing software tools.

As I always put it, there are four basic steps to editing a YouTube video!

Choosing the right video editing tool

You would be using the video editing tool to blend individual video shots into a single video which would later be uploaded to YouTube. The software would help you add special effects, graphics and onscreen texts on your video. There are a few low-cost editing tools which can offer good quality results. I personally use the licensed version of VideoPad, and that suffices the needs of YouTube videos.

Editing the video

Whatever editing tool you choose to go with, the basic action is simple, that is you will be attaching the individual video shots you have taken to make it a whole video. The aim is to come up with a video that looks smooth and effectively presents whatever you have got to say. Most of the editing tools provide you a timeline display, upon which you can add the individual video shots. Every single shot is a standalone video file, and you will be adding these files onto the timeline of your main video. You can juggle with the shots, trim them and delete those which you think are not helping you. You can also include transitions between your shots, such as fades to provide your video a more professional outlook!

Adding special effects, graphics and texts!

After you are done blending multiple shots into a single video, you can beautify the video using special effects. For instance, many channels want to display their website URL which can be done by superimposing it on the screen. You may also want to add text layers which will act as subtitles throughout your video.

You can also choose to bring in graphics or pictures. You can use special effects like changing the video filters, splitting the screen and so on. Besides, you can also add some music in the background (more will be discussed further). You don't really have to be a professional to do all these since the editing tools will be very easy to use.

But what you should remember is that while the special effects may look tempting, do not go overboard and use them all. The fancy effects or the graphics onscreen must not take away the attention your core content needs. The effects must help you have a good narrative, and not come in the way of the narrative!

Selection of right file format

Once your video editing is done, you could create a final product file to upload on the YouTube site. YouTube will mostly accept all major formats of files, so it shouldn't make a difference what format you choose. But I would suggest to go with .AVI, .WMA or .MP4 formats which are supported by most editing tools.

While you are editing the video, you need to ensure you use the widescreen format ratio 16:9 which the viewers are generally used to. Also, regardless of the format of the file you choose, you must render your video in either 1080p high definition or at least 720p. Though some of the viewers may wish to watch your video in a lesser resolution, it is suggested that you at least begin with 720p in your original file. This is because few of them might be watching your video on high definition TVs, big screens, and you wouldn't want to give them a video with poor resolution!

Even if you have recorded your video using your Smart phone, the quality of the editing will speak volumes about how professional your YouTube channel is. And people like videos that look professional in their editing. These four simple steps that I have mentioned above must be enough to begin with your YouTube videos.

18. YOUTUBE AUDIO LIBRARY - RIGHT MUSIC FOR YOUR VIDEOS!

Music is an integral part of your YouTube video unless it is you who is singing or playing instruments in the video. Adding background music was earlier a pain area because of the copyright guidelines. The risks were higher of your channel being striked off for using some other music without rights. YouTube decided to make it easy and simple for you by providing legal and free music which you can use in your videos.

Yes, I'm talking about the YouTube Audio Library!

YouTube Audio Library

The Library offers sound effects and royalty free music which you can use anywhere you wish to. Using these music is the simplest way to ensure your video doesn't face copyright infringement issues.

The Library doesn't just offer royalty free music but also inform you about the popular songs that are ad supported, and how you can use them in your videos. There are various tracks and sound effects. Here's some detailing on these.

Attribution of your videos: If you see attributions requisite icon next to a music track, ensure that you credit the original artist in the YouTube video description.

Monetizing your video: You can monetize your videos as the free music aren't claimed. If you're asked to show that you have the commercial rights to use the music, ensure you have the exact music title you got from the YouTube Audio Library!

Well, that's about it! That is how you can use music without worrying about copyright infringements!

19. USING END SCREENS AND YOUTUBE CARDS FOR EFFECTIVE VIEWERSHIP!

End screens and YouTube cards are the features in YouTube which you get to use while you are uploading your video, and these features will lead your viewers to other of your videos or playlist/channel/approved links from the video that they would be watching. You can use this on all your videos, thereby retaining your audience for a longer time in your channel. So, what is the big deal about it? I will tell you.

End screens and YouTube cards give the audience a Call To Action which will make your channel very effective in terms of converting the viewers into loyal fans. If you look at it, YouTube is a huge fan nurturing tank! Your goal must not be just to get people to click on your video but also to retain them until the whole video finishes.

Let's dissect this. Initially, you gain YouTube traffic that is people who have landed upon your video through search results or suggestions. Yes, it is amazing that they are watching your video of millions of videos out there, but such views would not be worthy in the long run if those viewers don't get converted into fans - Those who would come back to your channel when they feel the need!

Here is where Call To Action jumps into the picture, and this is where End Screens can be helpful!

First of all, what is Call To Action?

It is nothing but a straight request to your fans asking them to take certain actions further. It could be requesting them to subscribe to the YouTube channel, comment, like, share, follow on social media or watch something else from your channel or other channel!

Besides having effective titles, tags and thumbnails, including Call To Action in your videos is a great way to obtain your seasoned subscribers to stay engaged, and also to obtain new viewers!

If you think asking your viewers to do something could be slightly awkward, let me tell you why it is important to go ahead and do it.

YouTube is full of distractions, and many viewers would just move on once they are done watching your video. If you lose them like this, there's a possibility they may not find your channel ever again. While it appears to be simple, just seeking some Action is more than enough to get your viewers to do it. Hence, be particular about what you need them to do, and how you can keep up with the promise that you would be making.

And End Screens and YouTube cards are two simple ways to include Call To Action in your YouTube videos!

End Screens

This is a very efficient Call To Action which is available for you to use! They are basically screens which you can place at the end of your YouTube videos, to be specific they are displayed in the last 20 seconds, asking people to watch other videos or playlists from your channel/other channel or subscribe to your channel. If a viewer has reached the end of your video, it means that he/she was dedicated enough, and hence, you need to ensure there is a Call To Action displayed before them!

Earlier, you had to place End Screens with video editing and annotations, but now it is made easy through an easy feature embedded into the Video Uploader on YouTube.

To begin with, you must decide what the purpose of your End Screens are. You must always include a Subscribe button. What relevant videos you should direct them to is something you must decide. You can have a maximum of Four end screens, and to use them smartly is your job to do!

Now, it is time for you to upload your video on YouTube. In the edit mode, open the End Screens and annotations tab and add whatever elements you've chosen to add, and make sure you time them aptly. You could use the templates the YouTube offers, or also choose to drag and drop all those elements you need to include!

YouTube Cards

Well, you could call it a revised version of (and not as annoying as) Annotations! The plus point here is that YouTube cards work on Smart phones! You can add YouTube cards which would route your viewers to another playlist or video, your website or even other channels!

While you are using YouTube cards, the most important thing you got to do is to make it relevant. You must choose only few number of cards per video and you should get them to pop up at the right moment so that there are higher chances of your viewers clicking on it.

For instance, if you are putting up a Cover video, you can include a card suggesting the viewers to watch yet another cover of yours which falls in a similar niche. Make sure the card pops during the final moments of your video so that people don't move away from the current video early on and engage themselves with your channel after the video has ended.

Whenever you are uploading videos, see to it that you have added these Call To Actions. They are very easy to set up, and can effectively make an impact on your YouTube channel! Because the whole purpose is to develop a certain loyal fan base for your channel, while also pulling in more and more viewers to turn into subscribers! Remember, All is well that Ends well!

20. MONETIZE YOUTUBE CHANNEL WITH GOOGLE ADSENSE

Now that you have a YouTube channel that is up and running, the next obvious step is to monetize it. I mean, when you are already getting views and people are admiring your work, it is also obvious that you will be paid for your efforts! But how do you monetize your videos? Well, let me take you through one of the most important steps in having a YouTube channel!

The easiest method of monetizing your YouTube videos is through the enabling of Monetization option through your YouTube account, and linking it with your Google AdSense account.

Google AdSense by Google helps website publishers and YouTube video makers earn money from the content they are creating. Being a YouTube creator, you gain access to the publisher program from where you can start making money. Of all other monetizing ways, Google AdSense is the easiest and the most common way!

After you have linked your YouTube channel to your AdSense account, you will get the option of submitting your YouTube videos for monetization.

Your channel will be qualified for monetization only if it surpasses the monetization requisites of YouTube.

Earlier, if you had 10,000 lifetime views you'd be qualified for the YouTube Partner program. Now, there are new regulations in place. The channel must have a watch time duration of 4000 hours in 12 past months and 1000 subscribers at minimum. This is to set the non-committed

Youtubers away, and I don't think why it should affect you in any way.

Now that I have shared the monetization criteria, I would also like to tell you that you don't have to wait all the way until you reach the requisite criteria to enable the monetization option. You can rig up your settings now, and once the criteria is met, your channel will automatically be processed for monetization. Here is what you must be doing!

Open your YouTube dashboard by clicking on the YouTube account icon and then Creator Studio.

- Reach the Monetization page below the channel menu on the left sidebar.
- Below the 'Guidelines and Information' section, you will get information on 'How will I get paid?'
- Click on the AdSense association page, follow the immediate step which will lead you to the YouTube and AdSense association page.
- Sign in with that Google account that has got AdSense enabled, the account which you wish to associate with the YouTube channel.
- After you have logged in, choose 'Accept the association' on that page
- Next, you will be redirected to your YouTube channel account and will receive messages and notifications soon to enable Monetization for videos.
- Once you have logged in, click to Accept the association on the page.
- You will now be redirected to your YouTube account and soon receive message and notifications of enabling monetization for your videos.

After these steps, you will be eligible for enabling the monetization for each video that you have uploaded already. Besides, while uploading new ones, you get to choose if you would want to monetize the video or not. But what you must remember is that the actual monetization happens only after your channel has met the monetization criteria!

You can also enable monetization for all your future videos by selecting Monetize with ads under Channel → Upload Defaults

Choosing the Ad formats for your videos

You will be allowed to choose from all of the ad formats that are available, which will in turn decide the kind of ads that will be appearing in the YouTube videos.

Here is a list of the available Ad formats

- **Display ads** - These ads appear on the right side of YouTube videos if you're on PC

- **Overlay ads** - These ads appear on the lower end of YouTube videos

- **Skippable ads** - These are full-fledged video ads which play before the video and can be skipped after five seconds

- **Non-Skippable ads** - Non-skippable video ads cannot be skipped and can be displayed before your video can be viewed or during the video or after the video ends.

- **Sponsored cards** - Display cards with products feature in your video, on both mobile screens and desktop screens

21. GETTING PAID THROUGH ADSENSE

People usually ask me about how AdSense pays money. So, I've chosen to write a chapter about it which will give you better clarity on the subject.

To begin with, before you get paid through AdSense, you must be setting up the payment information correctly!

- Correct postal address which you'll be required to confirm later
- Give in tax information (not applicable to all the countries)
- Choose the payment method

If you have already opened your AdSense account and have already started including ads in your videos, AdSense will hold your money until all the details have been filled in correctly and postal address being verified. Besides, they send frequent notifications until you have verified all data.

When will I receive payments?

AdSense will always calculate the income for the span of a month. In the starting of the coming month, they review and calculate whatever you have earned. Around 21st of the coming month, AdSense will begin sending payments. Depending on the method of payment you have chosen, the time taken for the money to reach you differs. It is usually 2 hours to 10 days if you have chosen bank transfers.

What is the threshold of payment?

The payment threshold means the minimum amount of money you should have earned before getting paid. If you have just earned $50 in a month, you would not receive any payments. If you have earned $95 the next month, your total earnings would be $145 and you would be eligible for payment via AdSense. Basically, your earnings must have crossed $100 in order to receive payments.

While the payment threshold is likely the most important aspect for you, there are three more thresholds linked with earnings in AdSense. They are:

- Address verification threshold – Only after crossing $10, you will be able to complete address verification
- Selection of payment method threshold – After crossing $10, you can set the payment method

These details have to be mandatorily filled and verified if you want to receive payments.

What should I do if I do not receive my payments?

If you have already completed and verified your payment information, your entire income is more than the payment threshold and your payment has been due for over a month, and there is no issue mentioned in your AdSense dashboard, you can request re-issuing of the payment from AdSense. But in past 5 years I have not faced this issue.

Also check in AdSense account if the payment has been made, if yes, and still you have not received then contact your respective bank on why it's not credited to your account. This has happened to me couple of times as Bank guys wanted to know how is this money coming to your account. You may have to send an email to Bank mentioning the source of the earning.

What about the taxes on the AdSense income?

If your country is already collecting taxes, they would not make an exception out of your AdSense earnings. The tax amount you have to pay is basically your income tax amount which would vary from country to country.

22. WHY QUALITY OF CONTENT MATTERS MORE THAN THE QUALITY OF CAMERA!

M any a time, I confront people who speak about how they aren't getting to shoot a high quality video to start their YouTube channel. And all I give them is my personal example. Our first video on 'How to boil egg in Microwave oven' in "Savita Benur" channel was of such low camera quality that I myself found it to be pathetic. But that video remains to be one of the most viewed videos from our channels.

The world needs quality content. It doesn't matter what camera you are shooting it from as long as the video is decent enough to be watched, and doesn't look like a 3gp video! Now, I'm not implying you should settle down to normal quality videos. You can always improve the quality of your videos as you continue your journey in making YouTube videos, but that shouldn't be a hindrance for you to make videos in the first place. Quality content rules everything else!

I am stressing on the point of Quality content elaborately because you are a Content producer now, now that you have decided to have a YouTube channel for yourself. Netflix and Amazon have evidently set an example by realizing the importance of original and quality content.

People get overwhelmed by heavy information, and get overly tempted if there are click bait titles/images. That doesn't mean we continue supplying mediocre content. The beauty of creating original quality content is that you will be set apart from the mediocre ones, and you will develop an audience base who is looking for such quality!

Do it because you want to do it!

Do not fall prey for misleading titles or click bait content. Rather, create something because you have the drive to. Say things in your video because your inner self wouldn't let you stay quiet! Go for authentic content marketing. Go for things which will change you, and the one who views your videos. Create content that connects to the viewers, earn your audience than go behind targeted ones!

Yes, social appeal for your content is vital. Search engines have to be fed with things that can bring you up in the rankings, or else your video will sink down into abyss. But why not set some principles to your video content that will give you a higher standard?

Your video should speak for you, and your brand must be developed on the grounds of vintage values like unmatched quality craftsmanship and viewer centric experiences! Your content must be one of its kind. Don't go for spinning videos, get busy being creative!

Before you decide to make a video, ask yourself these things:

- Why should I do what I am about to do?
- Can my video add value to the ones who are watching it?
- Does my video require much inputs?
- Will I be able to say about the subject more than anyone else can?

I know it works on a deeper level and doesn't look easy. It involves your yearning, long sleepless nights, finding answers for tough questions! But it will all be worth it if you come up with authentic content that will hook your viewers to your channel!

Now that I have told you what are the things you should be asking yourself, I am now going to share with you the things you should be telling yourself in order to create high quality content for your videos!

- Generating more views is vital, but it is not as vital as who my audience is!

- I would instead have niche audience that would love what I do, than an indifferent large herd!

- I must be revolting against low quality content and must be recognized for top quality content!

- I must stand out because I stand for something

- My work must inspire others

Remember, while click bait contents run fast, original quality content run far! It is always your content quality that people will get used to. Give them the best quality, and they will keep coming back to you for more! Which will also help in getting more views in the long run.

23. USING THE SECRET SUPERPOWER THAT A PLAYLIST IS!

For you, a playlist might just be a compilation of categorized videos. But for the owner of the channel, it is a different deal altogether! Playlists are an amazing feature that YouTube offers, but it is also the one that many video makers don't pay heed to! This is mostly because they do not understand the edge they can get if they have playlists! Now, I am going to tell you the benefits as well as methods of having a great playlist!

For people who do not have clarity on what a playlist is, playlists are a group of related videos which could be viewed in succession. You may have already come across these on YouTube! Initially, you may not understand how a playlist could benefit your YouTube channel, but that's exactly what I will be sharing with you!

Playlists: How can they benefit us?

1. Better rankings

I've already shared with you a few things about the ranking algorithm of YouTube. YouTube doesn't just consider the total duration people have stayed on your video, but also considers their entire session on YouTube after they have watched your video!

A playlist will let a person watch videos back to back without having to do anything. This will ensure they are spending more time on your channel, and also the long viewing session on the site! Thus, your playlists will be boosted higher by the watch time algorithm of YouTube!

2. More visibility

Playlists do not just show up on your channel page but also on search results of both YouTube and Google alike! They even show up on the suggested videos section! This means more visibility for your videos!

3. You can aim at new keywords

Since playlists are individual entities in themselves, they would also help you rank better using keywords which you would not have used in the individual videos!

4. You can hike the views of videos that are less watched

There is not at all a restriction on what videos you add into your playlist, they could be your own videos, or someone's else, or even a blend of both! This implies that you can blend popular videos which belong to other people with those of your less loved videos, therefore increasing the number of views as well as the watch time of that particular video!

How do I create an effective playlist?

Let's first see how to create a playlist, go to **YouTube Home page** and click on **Customize Channel**, then click on **Playlists section** and you should be able to see **New Playlist** to create one.

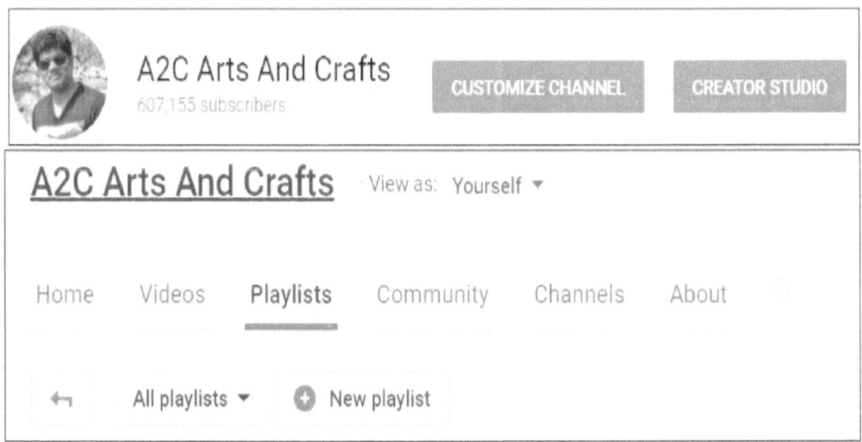

Now that you know how to create the Playlist the next obvious question is how to create an effective playlist! You would certainly want to reap in these benefits! Let me tell you, YouTube is as simple as it can get. Here is how you can create an effective playlist for your videos!

1. Introductory video

Well, I've started off with something that is not needed most of the times. But, if you think your playlist deserves some context, you could create an introductory video which is brief and which could tell people quickly what the playlist is all about! Also, YouTube now only allows you to choose one of the thumbnails of the videos in the playlist to be the thumbnail for the entire playlist. If you don't like thumbnails of the videos in the playlist, you can upload an introductory video with the thumbnail that you find perfect for the playlist!

2. Metadata

Optimizing your metadata is akin to how you probably would optimize your individual videos, only that you do not have much to optimize! You have to come up with a catchy description along with a catchy title for the playlist that would contain the keywords you wish to aim at. The thumbnail must be click worthy, while remaining relevant!

3. Promoting the playlist

All said and done, the final step is to promote your playlist in a similar fashion as that of your individual videos! You share it on your social media profiles, channel pages and the like! Besides, you must also update the playlist since every time a video is added to the playlist, it appears in the feed, giving all the more exposure! (That Rhymed!)

4. Define rules to auto add the video to playlist.

If you are uploading related videos to a Playlist, then you can define rules for videos to be automatically added to this playlist. Videos that fall under this rule will be automatically added to the playlist.

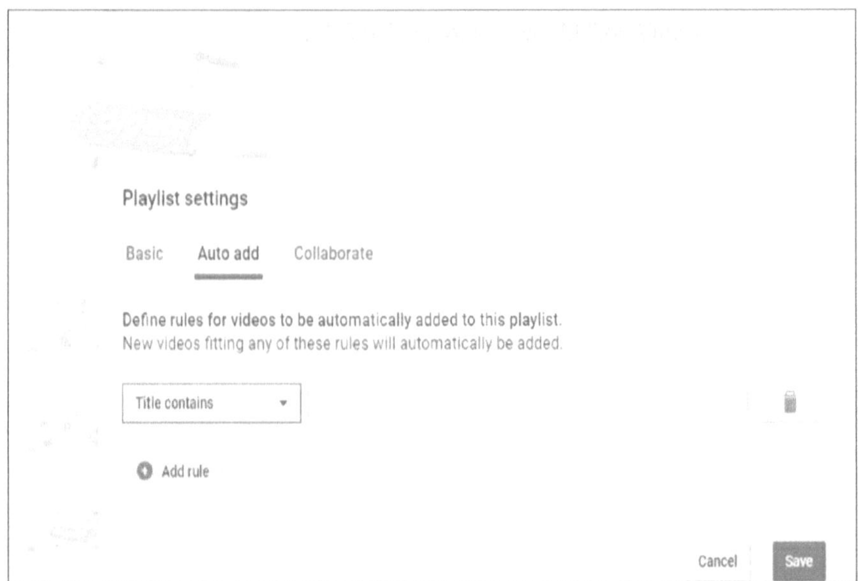

Well, that is how you create an effective playlist!! Playlist is that superpower of a YouTube channel which the channel owners don't bother unleashing! But when done right, your videos will rank up high like Flash!!

24. WATCH TIME CONCEPT

One of the most important factor deciding how much one can earn through the Google AdSense Program. By now you've learnt that YouTube pays 55% of its total revenue generated by displaying ads on the videos uploaded by the YouTubers, as on July 2018. The amount is calculated based on the views generated by a video or the entire channel as a whole. In the last chapter, we also learnt that the total revenue generated per 1000 views also depends on the location of the viewers of your videos and many other factors. So, does that lead us to a conclusion that the more number of views a channel has, the more the channel is going to earn? The answer is NO. YouTube earnings from Google AdSense depends *largely* on the number of views but it's not the sole factor at all! The most important thing that decides how much one can earn from YouTube is the total watch time of the channel which I'm going to discuss in detail in this chapter.

The most successful YouTubers or YouTube stars and "Wanna be" YouTube stars focus largely on increasing the watch time of the channel. Increasing the number of views in order to earn more is an outdated goal since 2012 and now every aspiring YouTuber struggles to increase the watch time of his or her channel. So what exactly is "Watch time"? And why is it so important?

Let's go back to the history......... (No, not the 19th century.. just a little back in time) Until the year 2012, view count was considered as one of the major factors that determined how much a particular earned. It was the primary measure that decided the success of a particular YouTube channel. With this concept, many people who published genuine content took a harsh beating because of their fraudulent competitors who drove more views to their channel by employing unethical means of getting more views. Spammy video titles and misleading thumbnails were used by the fraudulent video creators and they still earned good money for the sole reason that they had more views! Such videos managed to high views but the audience retention with the video was less and the bounce rate was very high which was a clear indication that the user was not at all satisfied with what the YouTube had suggested them. Can't blame it on YouTube because Little did YouTube know about the poor-quality videos as their only quality deciding factor was the number of views and YouTube showed all those videos with highest views as 'Suggested videos' This was a bad sign for YouTube and its reputation (And of course the earnings too)

Soon YouTube realized that the view count was not the most efficient factor that decided the quality and relevance of the video. It was, in fact, at most times very misleading. On the other hand, how much time a viewer is spending on the video is a far better measure that of viewers' satisfaction levels and relevance and quality of the video. At the end of the day, YouTube wants such content on its website that accelerates its users to stay on the YouTube website for longer time, thus leveraging more advertisers and in turn more business to YouTube. In a nutshell, what's more important to YouTube is the total watch time of a video and NOT the number of views. So your primary goal must be to increase the watch time of your videos and not just the number of views!

Furthermore, in the month of October 2012, YouTube updated its algorithms in a such a way that the videos having more watch time are favored by YouTube and it released an official update stating: "We've started adjusting the ranking of videos in YouTube search to reward engaging videos that keep viewers watching. The experimental results of this change have proven positive – less clicking, more *watching. As with previous optimizations to our discovery features, this should benefit your channel if your videos drive more viewing time across YouTube."*

Getting back to the question now.... *What* is 'Watch-Time' in YouTube?

Watch Time, according to YouTube, is *"The amount of time in aggregate that your viewers are watching your videos..."* And, according to the YouTube Creator Playbook, *"YouTube optimizes search and discovery for videos that increase watch time on the site"*.

Put it simply, watch time is a measure of how much your video contributed to a users' overall time watching videos on the site. For most of you, this wasn't so simple. Don't worry, I'll make it more simple for you. And it's crucial for you to understand what is watch time because, come on, I just said that it's the most important factor that determines the earning potential of your channel. To understand *what is* watch time better, we need to first understand *what is not* watch time.

Watch time is NOT just a measure of how much time a viewer has spent watching your video or how much percentage of your video is watched by a viewer. Dragging a content that can be completed in 5 minutes to around 20 minutes hoping the watch time of your video will be increased will not do much good to your channel because audience seek *genuine* content. And thus, watch time is really not just about how long people are watching your videos.

There are two important things that needs to be considered while discussing about the watch time:

Number 1 - Estimated minutes watched and the audience retention rate – Watch Time

Audience retention rate is measured by the average amount of time an individual viewer has spent in watching your video(s). The total estimated minutes watched by a viewer throughout is of greater importance here. A high audience retention rate indicates that that particular video is able to hold the audience's attention and the chances of such videos to be selected for 'Suggested videos' are high! And what follows? These videos will have greater watch time thus leveraging more income for you.

Number 2 - Session time or Viewer specific watch time

The viewer specific watch time is the total time spent by an individual user on YouTube who first came in search of your video and then moved on to watch other videos (it can be videos uploaded by other channels as well) The more time spent on YouTube by an individual user, the better it is for YouTube! So, if your video is leveraging other videos and thus helping in retaining a particular user on YouTube, the session time of your channel is high and YouTube favours such videos (For example: By getting these videos listed in 'Recommended videos' or 'Suggested videos') and that's in the best interests of the content creator!

So, in a nutshell, watch time is total minutes of videos watched on your channel by the viewers and Session watch time is total time someone stays on YouTube watching YouTube video.

Let's consider 2 examples here in relation to the total earnings made by a channel:

X video has 5 lakh views and is of 10 minutes duration, whereas Y video has only 3 lakh views with 20 minutes duration. Generally, going by the number of views one would say that X video is performing better as it has 2 lakh more views as compared to the Y video. (This is the old way in which YouTube worked before 2012 where view count mattered the most) But is the case so? NO. Look at the math below.

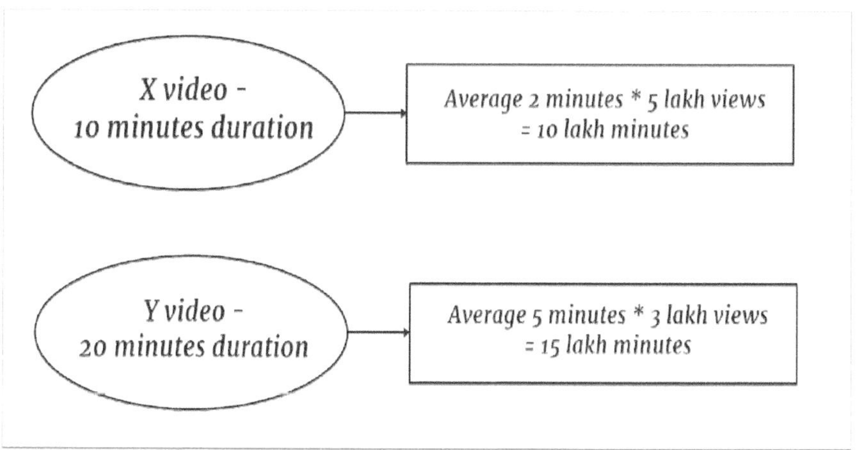

Thus, it can be noted that although, X video seems to be performing well, in reality, Y video is performing better than video X by generating more watch time and thus more income. Thus, you can make it a thumb rule that the more the watch time of a channel, the more number of ads are displayed and the more money a channel will be making.

So, it's very clear that utmost attention and importance must be given to increasing the overall watch time of your videos rather than just pushing the number of views generated. But how do you exactly increase the watch time of your YouTube channel? I've only listed down some here (Since I've given detailed explanations on each of these suggested tips in different chapters)

- How to increase the watch time of your videos?
- First things first - Create engaging and interesting content
- Unleashing the power of playlists
- The right title and thumbnail for videos
- Using 'Call-To-Action' End Screens/annotations
- Building up more and more subscribers
- Good editing skills to improve the quality of your video

25. HOW MUCH DO WE GET PAID FOR 1000 VIEWS?

I've explained how YouTube works in the previous chapters and how people can earn from it, trust me there are YouTube creators who have been earning in millions/year. Let me brush upon that a little so you can relate well to this chapter. Advertiser companies pay YouTube or Google for showing their ads on different YouTube videos and YouTube in turn pays 55% of its total revenue to the YouTubers who are the content creators.

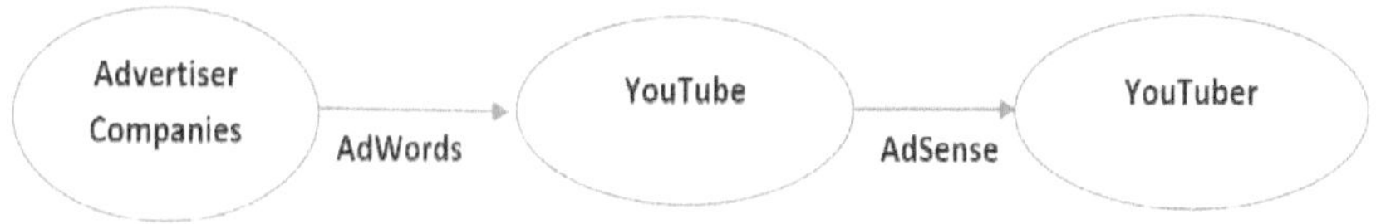

The next question that comes up is 'How much do we get paid for 1000 views?' There's no exact figure for this question as this depends on a number of factors. Before explaining the different factors that decides the amount earned per 1000 views let me tell you that there are many different ways of earning money from YouTube and here I'm only referring to the money earned by using the Google AdSense Program. Other ways of earning money from YouTube do not largely depend on the number of views generated by it. But when it comes to earning through Google AdSense, views/Watch time matter the most! You may say that the more views your videos are getting rather watch time, the more money you'll be making through the Google AdSense. Having clarified that, now let me tell you how much money can one expect for every 1000 views generated on the channel.

The amount paid per 1000 views mainly depends on the location of the viewers, type of ad displayed, duration of the video i.e. videos above 10 minutes can have multiple ads and videos below 10 minutes will have just one ad displayed. For example, talking about location of viewers: If you have large number of audience from United States, you'll be earning around 5 US dollars per 1000 views, whereas if you're audience is from India, you'll be making around 1 US dollar per 1000 views generated. So, the total revenue generated per 1000 views will be the sum total of earnings generated from audience scattered in different parts of the world. So, the amount paid per 1000 views largely depends on who are your major audience or viewers? Here's a small chart explaining the money generated per 1000 views when your audience belong to the following countries:

Nation	Approximate Money earned per 1000 views (In US dollars)
British Virgin Islands	$35
US	$5
India	$1
Few other countries	<$1

So that's a small brief on how much you can expect to earn per 1000 views. Again as I told you already, your gross earnings depends largely on the total watch time of your channel. Put it simply, it's more profitable for YouTube if your videos are of long duration where your audience is engaged in the whole or at least 70% of the video because that helps in increasing the chances of ad display on your videos! So, in a nutshell, you must remember that the more time your audience is spending in watching your videos, the more you'll be earning per 1000 views. Having 10,000 views for a video that's 5 minutes long is always better than having 20,000 views for a video that's 1-minute long. (I've covered this concept of watch time in detail in the previous chapter) So it's not entirely true that the more views you have, the more you can earn! It *largely* depends on the total time spent by a viewer on your videos than the number of viewers who clicked on your video!

26. TYPES OF YOUTUBE VIDEO ADS

As a YouTuber, what matters the most for you is to keep your channel running with the most interesting and engaging content that'll keep the viewed hooked on to your videos (And that of other videos too, which increases the session time of the channel) But you also need to have a fair knowledge about the different types of YouTube ads displayed. A detailed explanation isn't very crucial for people who generate content as opposed to the companies that must take a call on what type of advertisement they need on YouTube videos. Again, as I've already told you in the initial chapters of this book, Google ads are not the only way of earning from YouTube, it is *one of the ways* of earning through YouTube.

Major Types of YouTube video Ad formats

Non-Skippable video ads :

As the name suggests these ads cannot be skipped, ads must be watched before the video can be viewed. These ads can appear before, during, or at the end of the video.

These ad videos will not have 'Skip-Ad' option and thus there are chances that viewers bounce back from your video. But it doesn't mean everyone is going to do that. However, the earnings for these ads is on a higher side.

Skippable video ads:

Skippable video ads allow viewers to skip ads after 5 seconds, if they choose to do so. Ads can be inserted before, during the video, or at the end of the video.

Display ads:

These ads appear on the right side of the video being played and above the video suggestions list. The earnings on these type of ads is comparatively lesser than Skippable and non-skippable ads.

Overlay ads:

These are semi-transparent overlay ads that appear on the lower 20% portion of your video.

Like Display ads, the earnings on these type of ads is comparatively lesser than Skippable and non-skippable ads.

Bumper ads:

Non-skippable video ads of up to 6 seconds that must be watched before your video can be viewed.

Sponsored cards:

Sponsored cards display content that may be relevant to your video, such as products featured in the video. Viewers will see a teaser for the card for a few seconds. They can also click the icon in the top right corner of the video being played to browse the cards.

27. HOW TO GET 100 SUBSCRIBERS IN A DAY?

Having more subscribers will help you in generating more views as there's a ready audience for every new video you upload. Well, I'm sure all of you are aware of this now. But the true challenge lies in getting those first 100 subscribers. These first 100 subscribers are the ones who'll bring you more views for your initial videos and then the views will slowly start flowing to you automatically by snowball effect. It won't be as difficult to generate more views as it would be in the initial stages. So don't get disheartened when your videos aren't generating more views. You have to wait for your channel to kick off and getting those 'first 100 subscribers'! Many YouTubers struggle very hard in this very step of getting 100 subscribers and what's their action plan? Wait for it to happen! But let me tell you it's not that difficult at all to generate these minimum number of subscribers. In fact, you can get 100 subscribers to your channel on the very day when you've uploaded your first video on your channel! I'll tell you how to do it. (P.S.: For those of you who're thinking something might be fishy, let me tell you I'm going to tell you how to get your *first* 100 subscribers in a single day in the most ethical approach!)

Here's what you need to do in order to get the first 100 subscribers to your channel in a day:

Number 1 - ASK your close circle to subscribe to the channel personally!

I always ask people at my YouTube for Beginners session, "If you don't promote your channel, who else will?" No matter what you think about your videos, you should feel NO SHAME in asking your close circle friends and family members to subscribe to your channel.

I am sure everyone of us have at least 200 friends be it Mobile contacts, Facebook, WhatsApp, Instagram etc. If not, I would wonder where this person on planet lives (If you fall under this category, its high time to increase your friend circle).

Now get rid of your thinking patterns that says you've probably not given your best or the quality of your video could have been better and so on! Everyone feels that way in the beginning, but it doesn't mean you shy away from asking your friends and family members to subscribe to your channel. ASK and you shall get is a famous belief among the ancient Jews! Asking is your first and fundamental duty. Ask your colleagues, friends, people you know in your gym, neighbours and so on to subscribe to your channel. Call up your friends who you don't meet every day and ask for hem them to subscribe. Ensure that your close circle must turn into subscribers of your YouTube channel! Leave no stone unturned in this regard.

Number 2 - Sending personal messages on social media networking platforms

It's the age of social media networks and we're all aware of the power of social media. Biggest YouTubers earning millions of dollars are strongest with their social media promotions. Sending personal messages to all your Facebook friends is a great way to increase the number of subscribers to your channel. Send the link of your first video and ask them to support you by subscribing to your channel! Also, ensure that you use the right words. Instead of saying, "This is my new channel. Please subscribe to it", write something interesting like, "This was my first step towards my passion. Please do support me in this endeavor by subscribing to my channel" Get creative and innovative in asking people to subscribe to your channel. Get as many subscribers as possible from different social media networking platforms including Facebook, WhatsApp, Twitter and so on.

Number 3 - Include a Call-To-Action at the end of your video

After finishing your video, ensure that you have a Call-To-Action at the end where you're asking your viewers to subscribe to your channel by saying, "If you enjoyed this video, please like and share it. Also subscribe to it for not missing any updates" and so on. This Call-To-Action in your first video will help you get more views!

That's how simple it is to get the first 100 subscribers to your channel! Remember that, "You should be the first person to talk and promote your channel!" Feel no hitch in being the brand ambassador of your channel! Because if you don't believe in your channel, there's no reason why others should!

28. HOW TO GET MORE AND MORE SUBSCRIBERS?

As I've already told several times in this book, getting more subscribers to your channel is very important. In fact, any YouTube guide will tell you that. But the real question is How to get more subscribers to your channel? Now that you know how to get the first 100 subscribers to your channel, the next step is to learn how to keep up the consistency in the number of people subscribing to your channel. With over a billion visitors per month, there's a fairly large potential audience for every uploaded video on YouTube. But it totally depends on how you can get these people subscribe to your channel. Many YouTubers go wrong in completing this most important step. The content that's great isn't just enough for the success of a YouTube channel in the long run. Because great content can generate more views but how to ensure that these visitors who showed interest in your videos stay hooked on to your channel? By getting them subscribe to your channel! Here's how you can convert your viewers into subscribers of your channel and get more and more subscribers! Let's begin!

1. Produce engaging content

It goes unsaid that the very first step towards getting more and more subscribers is producing highly engaging content. If you want people to subscribe to your channel, you need to convince them that you're going to make videos that will interest them! This convincing is to be done and can be done only by producing the engaging content on a consistent basis! So what exactly is engaging content? In other words, how can you make your content engaging? There are 2 possibilities where the content can be engaging and all trending YouTube channels will fall under these 2 categories:

- Entertaining content
- Informative content

The content which works best is either an entertaining content or an informative one. But the content that *really* works the best are those which are **entertaining and informative!** So, if you can make your videos both engaging and informative, there's no stopping you from getting more and more subscribers to your channel. People have something to take home as well as entertain themselves while watching your videos in this case and there are high chances your viewers will subscribe to your channel. In a nutshell, videos that inform and entertain are the most successful ones with highest number of views and followers! So yeah, take a note of making your videos that are *really* engaging!

> *"The content which works best is either an entertaining content or an informative one. But the content that really works the best are those which are entertaining and informative!"*

2. Plan your videos (Script your videos) and channel

In the first chapter of this book, I've told that do not shy away from making videos thinking you don't have any experience. Everyone's got a start and you'll have yours too! But that doesn't mean you upload amateur videos consistently! You have to improve with the time and this improvement needs to be reflected in the videos you upload. Plan the videos carefully which will help you in making the best video with no scope for wastage. I'll tell you why it's important to focus on the planning of your video. People get drifted away from your video if you seem clueless on your video. Doing anything that makes your viewers bounce back from your videos is NOT good for your channel. Plan what you're going to upload and also plan what you're going to talk in these videos. Plan the structure of your channel and as I've already told, it's extremely important to create channel only after you have enough conviction on the niche you're going to target upon. Don't upload all types of videos on your channel, because this won't help your subscribers believe that your channel is of any value to them and thus they won't subscribe to your channel because they don't find a reason to!

> *"Remember that if you fail to plan the structure of your channel and videos, you're planning to fail in getting more subscribers to your channels."*

3. Maintain the consistency of your channel and slowly increase the uploading frequency

The very reason people subscribe to your channel is because they've liked your previous videos and want to see more such videos. Thus you need to maintain the consistency in uploading videos to your channel. Release your videos in a recurring, timely and a structured fashion. Uploading videos at a particular time during the day every week keeps your audience engaged and keeps them waiting for your videos. Most successful channels upload their videos at the same time every week. I usually upload on Sunday during 3PM to 7PM as the channel gets highest views during this time, which means most of my subscribers will be watching during this time. This is a great strategy to keep your audience engaged. Slowly, increase the frequency of uploading videos to your channel, say, if you've started to upload one video every month, slowly make it two a month and then four a month! This helps greatly in generating genuine number of interested subscribers to your YouTube channel.

4. Ensure that ASK your viewers to subscribe to your channel

I've told the importance of asking your viewers to subscribe to your channel in the last chapter. As much as it helps in getting your first 100 subscribers, it also helps in increasing the overall number of subscribers to your channel. Ensure that you ASK the viewers to subscribe to your channel either at the beginning or the end of the video. You can see that trending YouTubers today are coming up with most creative and innovative ways of asking viewers to subscribe to the channel! Get as creative as possible! Think outside the box or even better, think like there's no box at all!

5. Make use of 'Call-To-Action'

Make use of End Screens requesting for the audience to subscribe to your channel. End Screens are displayed during the last 20 seconds of your video and if your audience love your video, they would definitely subscribe to your channel!

6. End your videos on a high note

Just like the drama dialogues that take place just before the curtain falls creates the best and strong impression, same goes with your channel. Ending your videos on a high note and *then* asking your viewers to subscribe to your channel will get you maximum number of subscribers! Like people say, first impression is the best impression but the last impression is the long-lasting impression, it's very important to end your videos on high note! No matter what the content of your video is, the ending must be made memorable and should be crafted in such a way that it strikes a chord with the viewers!

> *"Like people say, first impression is the best impression, but the last impression is the long-lasting impression, it's very important to end your videos on high note!"*

7. Let your audience know that you acknowledge and appreciate their viewership

Everyone likes people who express gratitude and so do your viewers. Your viewers would be motivated to subscribe to your channel if you expressly tell that you really appreciate their viewership and you'd love more support from them! I guess now you know why many YouTubers say,

"Thank you so much for watching my video" It's a gesture of gratitude that'll surely pay you off!

8. Keep up the audience engagement

The viewers who watch your videos might comment on your videos and it's your duty to let them know that you're hearing and appreciate their comments. The loyal audience will definitely care for you if you show them that you care for them. You may see many viewers requesting you to upload a particular type of video in the comments section. This means that they are your loyal audience who wants to love and support you in your endeavor! Do make videos that are requested to the maximum possible extent. Needless to say that you'll also come across certain anger and backslashes in your comments section but you can always choose to only focus on your *loyal* audience! Reply to the comments and engage well with your viewers!

9. Have attractive thumbnails

Thumbnails is something similar to the teaser or trailer of your video. It's going to be the face of your video and you can get more clicks to your video if you have an attractive thumbnail. Thus, more views can be generated leading to more subscribers too! Keeping the thumbnail attractive and at the same time relevant and unique is the key here! Invest good amount of hours in making the best thumbnail for every video you upload.

10. Make your channel trailer appealing and attractive

When people view your videos for the first time and they're interested to know more about your channel, the first they're going to check out is the channel trailer uploaded by you on your homepage. If they find this trailer is going to add value to them either by entertaining them or by providing information, chances are good that they'll subscribe to your channel! Just like you book your tickets on different movie booking apps after watching the trailer of the movie. Thus, you need to ensure that this trailer effectively speaks about who you are, what you do and what your channel is all about! A short video of about 2 minutes is a good way to go to help your viewers know more about your channel. Remember that your video must be so effective that within a short span of 2minutes, it must leave a deep and long-lasting impact on what your channel is all about and how it adds values to your viewers!

These were some of the ways through which you can increase the number of subscribers to your channel! Following all these steps once in a while wouldn't suffice (Unless you want your subscribers to back off and unsubscribe from your channel) Consistency in following these steps is the key to get more and more subscribers as you progress!

29. CONSISTENCY IS THE CRYPTO!

M any YouTubers who have attended my seminar keep asking me how they can take their video to the next level and get more views. And I always tell them the same thing; Be consistent! It might be an age-old mantra for success in every field, but it still holds good and will continue to! Consistency is a multifaceted strategy that can be used to grow your YouTube channel. Consistency should not just be in your content but also in posting the videos so that your audience have got a purpose to visit your channel time and again!

How can consistency boost views?

Striking the balance between regular uploads and quality of the content could be tricky, even to a seasoned YouTuber! But YouTube certainly values those creators who upload videos regularly while managing their video quality consistent, and will bring in more traffic to these creators! So, the next obvious question is

How to maintain consistency?

There are two major ways you can maintain consistency as a YouTuber!

With your content

You might be a person with unique ideas, varied and wide range of interests! But let me be honest with you, YouTube isn't the place for showcasing these interests. When you develop certain content and associate yourself with that style because your audience has loved it, DO NOT FLINCH FROM THAT STYLE! Stick to your content so that your audience knows what they can expect when they visit your YouTube channel. When you build your content as a brand, you will be developing viewer loyalty!

And remember, convincing your loyal audience to watch your video is much easier than convincing a complete stranger!

Regularity

If your audience is fond of your channel, knowing when your video will come out is as essential as knowing what they can expect in your videos. Consider announcing when your next video will arrive and ensure that you stick to it. This way, you will be establishing certain trust with your viewers, and this will only increase your channel viewership!

Having said that, don't you think it all makes sense? Maintain consistency, and you will go a long way! Because Consistency is the Crypto for success on YouTube!

30. ONE VIDEO IS ENOUGH TO PICK UP THE CHANNEL

Don't worry if you are not getting great views in the beginning. You may have uploaded multiple videos, but just one video is enough to get thousands of views and thus increase your subscribers and overall channel views. So, stay focused and keep uploading the videos! All the very best!!